Motive or Motivation?

Donte' P. Brown

ACTIVATE PUBLISHING
CINCINNATI, OHIO

Motive or Motivation? © 2012 by Donte' P. Brown. All rights reserved. Printed in the United States of America. No part of this book may be used or reproduced, scanned or distributed in any printed or electronic form without prior written permission except in the case of reprints in the context of reviews. Please do not participate in or encourage piracy of copyrighted materials in violation of the author's rights. Purchase only authorized editions. For information, address Activate Publishing, P.O. Box 46728 Cincinnati, Ohio 45246-0728 or visit our Web site at www.motiveormotivation.com

Library of Congress Cataloging-in-Publication Data

Brown, Donte P.
Motive or Motivation? / Donte' P. Brown.
ISBN 978-0-9846107-1-6
LCCN 2012900097

This book is designed to provide information and motivation to the readers. This publication is not intended to render any legal or professional advice regarding the subject matter covered. It is sold with the understanding that neither the author nor the publisher are rendering psychological, legal or other professional services. If legal advice or other expert assistance is required, the services of a competent professional should be sought. The content of this book is the sole expression and opinion of its author, and not necessarily that of the publisher. No warranties or guarantees are expressed or implied by the publisher's choice to include any of the content in this book. Neither the publisher or the author shall be liable for any physical, psychological, emotional, financial, or commercial damages, including, but not limited to, special, incidental, consequential or other damages. Our views and rights are the same: You are responsible for your own choices, actions, and results.

The author has tried to recreate events, locales and conversations from his memories of them. In order to maintain their anonymity in some instances he has changed the names of individuals and places, he may have changed some identifying characteristics and details such as physical properties, occupations and places of residence.

ATTENTION: EDUCATIONAL AND PROFESSIONAL ORGANIZATIONS
Activate books are available at quantity discounts with bulk purchase for educational, business, or sales promotional use. Visit nawman11@gmail.com to schedule the author to speak at your next engagement.

Edited by: Monica Blackwell-Harper
Cover Art by: Donte' P. Brown

ACKNOWLEDGMENTS

First and foremost, I want to recognize my lord and savior Jesus Christ. It is wonderful to know that my GOD is one daddy who will never leave and has always been there whenever I have needed him. I am honored that GOD inspired me to write this book. I have come to understand how vitally important it is for those of us who are believers to cast our burdens on him and rely on his guidance as we maneuver through life.

I want to send a special note of gratitude to my *"mommy"*. Yes, I said *"mommy"*, here I am a 39-year-old man referring to his mother as *"mommy"*. I smile when I use this term to describe her because it brings back fond memories of the days when she held me in her arms and told me everything was going to be all right. My mother is one of the strongest people I have ever known. She has overcome so many of life's obstacles including; alcoholism, domestic violence, and cancer. Most of all she took on the challenge of raising three boys on her own. I can't thank you enough for never taking the coward's way out and leaving us. Despite all of our struggles, you stayed and played the role of both mom and dad. You helped instill the importance of family and showed us how crucial it is to continue to hope. Even though we did not have much we always had love. I must say that the biggest *motivation* in my life has always been the love that you have shown us. Without knowing I was loved by you and our family I know I would not have become the person I am today. Thank you for teaching me how to love. I'm grateful that you are my mother. I love you.

To my wife Chandra, I can't say enough about what you mean to me. You have helped me to be a better man. Your words of encouragement have continued to inspire me to strive for more and never give up. He who finds a wife finds a good thing. I believe he who finds a GODLY wife finds a great thing. I have found all of what I need in you; a friend, confidant, and partner. Thank you for your patience in helping me with this labor of love. Even when I was annoying and irritating you were there to hear my revisions. Without your resourcefulness and intelligence I am sure this book would not have come to be. I also want to thank you for being my co-pilot and sounding board in this journey of parenthood. Bless you for serving as the cradle of life for our two beautiful children. I pray that with GOD's help we will continue to be the parents that GOD wants us to be. You are a spectacular mother and I am so happy to have you to assist me with raising our children in the right way. I don't know if I love you says enough, but I truly do.

Thank you to my children, Trinity and Christian, for serving as excellent examples of how children should be. You both are well-mannered, studious, curious, bold, and strong. You both are wise beyond your years. As long as I shall live, you will never be *"daddiless"*. I truly hope that I can serve as the living role model for your lives. I pray that you will desire to emulate my positive characteristics and learn from my mistakes so that you will not make the same ones that I have. I promise to give you guidance and I truly pray that you trust in knowing that I will never encourage you to do anything that will hurt you. I will always have your well-being and best interests at heart in all that I do. You both are truly the joy of my life.

It is important that I take this time to acknowledge my two brothers Tony and David. Your missteps and successes have led the way for me. Your experiences made it possible for me to avoid many of the pitfalls of life. Thanks for the life lessons. Most of all, thanks for serving as daddies by default.

To my extended family of aunts, uncles, and cousin, you all deserve credit for being a great support system for me. Thank you all for your love and concern for our family. We have all grown together and it is fantastic to know that you will be there if I need you.

I can't say enough about my best friends Luis, Steve and Tyson. Each of you are true daddies in your own right. I thank GOD for bringing you guys into my life. After so many years of being friends, I have watched you all take on new challenges as daddies and all of this has been done in stride. None of you have missed a beat. I am proud to call you my brothers from other mothers. Thank you for your support and words of wisdom in addressing this important subject.

To my good friends the Harpers; Tramell, Monica and their children (Joshua, Nicholas and Gabrielle), I can't tell you how much I appreciate you all. First, I want to say thank you to Tramell for his patience in allowing me to take up so much of his wife's (Monica) time with this book. Next, thanks kids for loaning me your mother and giving up your spare time with her so that she could help me out with this project. Monica, I am grateful for all of the time and hard work you put into editing this book. I knew I chose the right person to assist me with this endeavor because of your intellect, honesty and your willingness to help others. The level of dedication and perseverance you have shown in hand writing your recommendations is enviable for even the most committed editor. You are a wonderful, kind-hearted mother who has wonderful qualities that should be imitated by other parents.

I want to recognize all of the mothers who have been raising their children on their own. We all have choices in life and you didn't have to stay but you did. You deserve recognition for your willingness to stick it out. I applaud you for not giving up.

Thanks to my Bishop, Victor S. Cousins and my Inspirational Baptist Church Family for serving as a source of spiritual refuge and peace in the midst of this chaotic world.

Finally, to my dad, Frank, thanks for having the courage to come back into my life. I commend you for making the effort to be there for me. I sincerely appreciate it.

For anyone I may not have mentioned, please charge the omission to my head and not my heart. GOD BLESS!

CONTENTS

THE PUZZLE	1
PRELUDE	4
Chapter I. **IF THEY CAN DO IT WHY COULDN'T HE?**	15
Chapter II. **CONCEPTION AND BIRTH**	21
Chapter III. **MOMMA'S BABY DADDY'S MAYBE**	27
Chapter IV. **GENERATIONAL CURSE**	33
Chapter V. **FINANCIAL SUPPORT**	39
Chapter VI. **THE MOTIVE**	48
Chapter VII. **WHAT WAS HIS MOTIVE FOR LEAVING?**	79
Chapter VIII. **BABY MAMA DRAMA**	88

Chapter IX.
THE TRAP   91

Chapter X.
TOO YOUNG, TOO SCARED, TOO MUCH RESPONSIBILITY   95

Chapter XI.
A WOMAN CAN'T TEACH A BOY HOW TO BE A MAN   100

Chapter XII.
DADDY BY DEFAULT   115

Chapter XIII.
THE WORLD OWES ME SOMETHING   119

Chapter XIV.
IDENTITY CRISIS   124

Chapter XV.
I'M A MAN   136

Chapter XVI.
DYSFUNCTION AND DISCONNECTION   143

Chapter XVII.
WHAT IF THEY'RE BOTH GONE   150

Chapter XVIII.
IT'S LIKE HE WAS DEAD TO ME   158

Chapter XIV.
ON THE FRINGE   164

Chapter XX.
MISSED OPPORTUNITIES   170

Chapter XXI.
FORGIVENESS AND HEALING (THE
MOTIVATION)   174

Chapter XXII.
WHAT MOTIVED ME?   182

Chapter XXIII.
EASILY INFLUENCED   215

Chapter XXIV.
"WHAT IF?"   223

Chapter XXV.
SO WHAT "MOTIVATES" YOU?   226

Chapter XXVI.
DISCIPLINE, SACRIFICE, AND PATIENCE   229

Chapter XXVII.
INSPIRATION COMES FROM WITHIN   234
AND FROM DOING WITHOUT

Chapter XXVIII.
MY FATHER CHANGED MY LIFE 237

MOTIVE OR MOTIVATION

THE PUZZLE

Yesterday I woke up and realized I was a man.
No one was there to guide me and I did not understand,

What it meant or how to be or what was all involved
I knew it was a puzzle that one day I'd need to solve.

I looked at what's made up my life and all that it has been,
Exploring all the different things that change us boys to men.

I examined who I'd come to be the turns that brought me here,
The pieces just don't seem to fit confirming my worst fear.

The thing that I had feared the most was right there in my face,
The fear of failing as a man the stigma of my race.

Portrayed as deadbeat dads and losers who refuse to work
Or criminals and thugs and pimps or simply outright jerks.

Who abuse and hurt our women and abandon our kids,
Or show up and try to play dad in between the jailhouse bids.

But what about me? The man I am, confused about my role?
I paid the cost to be the boss but forgot to pay the toll?

There is no way, this is not true, I've stepped up to the plate
I've done the things my dad did not and I wasn't thirteen years late.

I guess what I am trying to say and in no way am I dissing,
But how can you complete the puzzle when there's a piece (peace) that's missing.

The piece (peace) that I'm referring to is essential to be a man,
But many men deny this fact and proceed the best they can,

To go through life without this piece (peace) but the puzzles incomplete
Some do learn to live without and others simply compete.

But still there will remain a void no matter how hard you try.
You'll always wonder what made him leave and you still want to know why.

But as I pondered, thought it through, exploring who I am
I wondered since my dad was gone if he really gave a damn.

Since he wasn't there to guide me through most of my early years
He wasn't there to comfort me to wipe away my tears.

He wasn't there for my first hit or my first football game
I wonder if he had been there would my life have been the same.

I couldn't tell you where he lived or the kind of work he does
I could have walked right by the man and wouldn't have known who he was.

You may be quite dysfunctional and don't know what to do,
The things that you see your father do, all help to make you, you.

As complex as this thing may be you may not ever know
That all the things you hear and see are the things that help you grow.

But if you never hear from him you cannot emulate
The things he does, the things he says, the ways he may be great.

But then again the things you miss may make you better still
Because you won't pass on his faults and leave a void unfilled.

For some the chance to meet their dad may come with great elation
The fact that he wasn't always there can be a *motive* or a *motivation*.

PRELUDE

Fatherless v. Daddiless

First, I would like to begin by providing an explanation of the premise of this book. Throughout history, there have been a variety of studies that have addressed the impact that growing up fatherless can have on a child. Many of these studies outline the problems that can result when a man decides he cannot or will not fulfill his fatherly duties. Obviously, the absence of a father can result in some dramatic consequences for their children. My objective in writing this book was to take a practical look at the things that can compel a father to be a *"no show"* for their child's life. At the same time, I wanted to help fatherless children address their feelings and recognize that it is possible to overcome the stereotypes associated with being without their fathers.

As I embarked upon penning this book, I contemplated the meaning of the word *"father."* One definition was handed to me on Father's Day about two years ago. My children presented me with a glass desk placard with the definition of *"father"* etched into it. The glass paperweight described *"father"* as *"a male parent; one who loves, supports, guides, inspires and encourages his children; a man of strong character who teaches by example; one who is patient, kind, and understanding; a man who is emulated, admired and very loved."* The definition ended with my name inscribed.

I sincerely appreciated the sentiment behind this gift and I believe I possess all of the characteristics it described, however when I thought about the definition I did not feel it was completely accurate. What I mean is, while everyone has a father not all of them possess the previously described qualities. In fact, it really does not take much to be a father. Technically, a deposit at the local sperm bank can result in a man obtaining that title. I believe the attributes on my desk weight personified the characteristics of a *"daddy"*, not just a *"father"*. The term *"daddy"* evokes feelings of love and closeness; the word is widely regarded as a term of endearment. So unless you live in a formal environment or in certain parts of the world, the term *"father"* is not what is usually heard when children race to greet their dad when he arrives home. Most children holler excitedly, *"DADDY!"*, when he comes into view.

Please understand that I know the words *"father"* and *"daddy"* essentially mean the same thing in the English language. My viewpoint is more a matter of perspective than it is about the formal definitions. I feel so passionately about what being a *"father"* really means that I think we should change what we call the day when we honor these men.

Maybe we should change *"Father's Day"* to *"Daddy's Day"* because in my opinion the word *"daddy"* more accurately describes the true meaning of what we are celebrating.

Moreover, it is ironic to me that people use the expression *"fatherless"* when they describe a child that has been abandoned by his or her father. The truth is, the child still has a *"father"* but he has chosen not to be in his child's life. Thus, a more appropriate way to describe the children caught in these situations is to refer to them as *"daddiless"*. As a result of my strong conviction and belief that anyone can be a *"father"* but not everyone has stepped up to the plate to be *daddy,* throughout this book, I frequently refer to these children as *"daddiless"* instead of *"fatherless"* because that is really what they are.

I truly hope this book will inspire hope and strength, as well as, encourage people to take charge of their lives by turning their *"daddiless" motive* into *motivation*. I also hope this book will serve as a catalyst to inspire a father or a child to open their heart and mind to healing. Helping them to understand that by using patience, perseverance, and having a positive attitude, anything can be accomplished. Inspiration to do what's right instead of allowing your circumstances to push you into doing something wrong is what this book is all about. Just like most things in life, there is a choice to be made as to how you will respond and being *daddiless* is no different. When pivotal moments happen in the life of a *daddiless* child they can be a turning point. The decision must be made as to whether their fathers absence will be a *"motive"* or a *"motivation"*.

MOTIVE VS. MOTIVATION

Let's look at the words *"motive"* and *"motivation"*. Just as the words *"father"* and *"daddy"* technically have the same meaning, similarly the words *"motive"* and *"motivation"* are spelled differently but have a common meaning. In fact, *"motivation"* is a derivative of the word *"motive"*. The question is, do they really mean the same thing in American society? By definition, the word *"Motive"* means *"something (as a need or desire) that causes a person to act (Webster Ninth New Collegiate Dictionary)"*. From a legal perspective, the *"Black's Law Dictionary"* defines the word *"Motive"* as the *"cause or reason that moves the will and induces action. An idea or belief or emotion that impels or incites one to act in accordance with his state of mind or emotion."* Alternatively the word *"Motivation"* is defined as *"a motivating force, stimulus, or influence."*

The two words appear to be very similar, as a common theme of *"action"* is threaded through both these definitions. Even the spelling of the words are very close. The thing is our society has perpetuated views of these two words that are very different. The societal viewpoint of these words is one of the reasons why I have included the criminal law definition. Society has created a belief that the word *"motive"* exemplifies something bad while the word *"motivation"* incites goodness. In a moment, I will explain my perspective on these two words as they relate to the topic of children growing up without their fathers. Most important is the fact that these two words provide the backdrop for this book.

When I evaluated the word *"motive"* in relation to *"daddiless"* children, I along with many people in American society considered the term to be negative. For example, in many instances when a person is found guilty of committing a crime, whether it is a violent or non-violent offense, one of the first points the lawyer will argue in mitigation of the sentence is the fact that the individual grew up without a father. I know this is true because in many of the cases I handled that is what I argued. The pleadings to the court that a child's *daddilessness* contributed to their criminal behavior helps to establish my viewpoint that when it comes to being *daddiless* the word *"motive"* is considered negative. Further, when a person does not seem to have good intentions in what they are doing, they are sometimes said to have an *"ulterior motive"*, meaning their original intentions were not actually the reason they did what they did. Ulterior motives are also a large part of why children become *daddiless*. For example, when many of these men laid down with these women their desire was not to have a long-term relationship. In some of these cases, the man's *"motive"* was simply to have sex. He never intended to stay with the child's mother. Thus, the unintended pregnancy may have revealed his true purpose. He may have lied to her claiming, for example, that he loved her, but in actuality he just wanted to have sex with her without a true commitment.

Alternatively, I considered the word *"motivation"* and I found that for some of us being *daddiless* can push us to work harder and to accomplish more. Thus, *"motivation"* has a positive connotation when it relates to most things in life. For example, a *"motivational speaker"* will attempt to help a person better themselves or to improve an aspect of their lives. For the most part, these individuals present positive influences to assist and inspire others to improve themselves or to take positive actions. If a situation or an action can push a person in the right direction this is the *"motivation"* that I am referring to.

I deliberated on how the words *motive* and *motivation* might apply to someone like me whose initial face-to-face meeting with his father occurred at the age of 13. I also thought about how these words might be attributable to other children like my two brothers who really do not know much about their father at all. I even evaluated what impact being *daddiless* might have on our sense of identity and how a need for acceptance might push us down the wrong path or instead help to drive us to become leaders.

Even though I met my father later in life, many of the feelings and circumstances I am writing about are as personal for me as they are to others who have never met their fathers. Based on my personal experience of being poor, black and *daddiless* I realized that the absence of this male figure could push you in either a negative way *(motive)* or positive way *(motivation)*. Some people find themselves midway between *motive* and *motivation,* while others find they are at the far end of either side of the spectrum.

I recalled some of the kids I grew up with not having their fathers in their lives as well. Each of us was without the person who is meant to be one of the biggest influences we were to have. We were abandoned, left to make life-changing decisions on our own or at least without our father's guidance. What is interesting is that the choices we made varied greatly. Because of our choices, some of us were "motivated" to become lawyers, accountants, stockbrokers and mail carriers. Other individuals allowed their *"motive"* to control their decisions and they became petty criminals, burglars, drug dealers and even murderers.

Even in my own household, the differing dynamics of not having a father present were manifested. On the one hand, the *motive* or negative effects were evident when my middle brother was sentenced to the Ohio penitentiary multiple times due to his committing burglaries to supply his crack cocaine addiction. Alternatively, m*otivation* was demonstrated by my eldest brother setting a positive example for me and my middle brother to emulate. He led the way for us two younger boys by being a responsible young man who took on a fatherly role and helped my mother take care of us financially and otherwise. Most importantly, my eldest brother graduated from college with a B.A. degree in psychology, an accomplishment that very few people in my extended family have been able to achieve. The fact he desired to pursue college at all was exceptional considering he did not have anyone in our household as an example that achieving a higher education was possible.

This is not to say that my eldest brother did not encounter some scrapes with the law; however, he turned his negative experiences into positive outcomes. My brothers presented two of the potential paths that lay ahead for me to travel. Crackhead or egghead, which one would I choose?

Fortunately, for me GOD helped me choose the latter path. GOD allowed me to experience various parts of both my brothers' lives. For example, I tasted alcohol at an early age but GOD took the taste of it out of my mouth so I never had to progress down the drug path that sometimes follows alcoholism. I witnessed first-hand the devastating effects that alcohol can have on a person's life. Only by GOD's grace did I remain on the drug-free side of the fence.

I was also fortunate that my eldest brother was six years older than I was. Therefore, when I was 12 years old he went off to college and I had an opportunity to visit with him there. Spending time with my brother on his college campus provided me with a fresh perspective that differed from the ghetto where I lived. Being exposed to higher learning motivated me to strive for more. Even though my father was not present as a role model, I had examples from my brothers that covered the spectrum of what I should and should not do.

The words *motive* and *motivation* may have varying connotations to different people. For example, some individuals who grew up without their fathers may exhibit the *daddiless motive* by displaying a blatant disregard for their fellow human beings. A person that has felt abandoned may take on the attitude *"it's every man for himself, this is a dog eat dog world where I've got to get mine before somebody else does."* This person may have little regard for anyone other than him or herself because they believe no one cared about them, so why should they care about anyone else. Typically, people who have this narcissistic attitude may harbor feelings that result in self-destructive behavior along with an inability to connect with others. I can relate to some of the feelings of animosity, anger, and frustration that these people feel. Many of these feelings are misplaced toward others when they are really meant to be exhibited toward their fathers.

Let me make a point of saying that by no means am I a psychiatrist or psychologist, nor am I attempting to dissect these situations from a psychoanalytical perspective. I have not conducted any formal studies, however, I am someone who has first-hand knowledge about feeling a variety of emotions, including at times hatred, for a person who did not seem to care at all about their innocent child's life. I want to emphasize the word *"innocent"* because the child did nothing to this man but be conceived and subsequently be born alive.

Conversely, at the other end of the scale are people who utilize the absence of their father as a *motivation to* accomplish positive pursuits, thereby achieving their goals. These children mature into adults who, because of their *motivation*, transform a negative situation into a positive one. We are the people who live by the philosophy *"when you have* lemons you make lemonade," turn the sour to the sweet. Using this negative as a positive, we have been able to overcome the hard times that we have had to face. We have made positive efforts to prevent these negative situations from happening in our lives again. Many of us have used this negative situation as a *"motivation"* to break the generational curses that are sometimes associated with being *daddiless*. We work harder to be the daddies we never had. Some *daddiless* people tend to work harder at nurturing relationships with their children and spouses to keep their families together, sometimes even to their detriment.

In this book, I also explored the differences between men and women who use *daddilessness* as a *motive* and those who allow it to be *motivation*. I began by examining some of the reasons fathers leave and I end by discussing some of the obstacles that I was able to overcome throughout my *daddiless* journey. As you read this book please note that in certain instances the pronouns *"he"* or *"she"* and *"his"* or *"her"* are not intended to be gender specific. Thus, if the information may be appropriately related to a male or female, please do not get caught up in the pronoun that is used within the sentence. Please keep in mind, this book is intended for any *daddiless* person regardless of their gender.

Chapter I.

IF THEY CAN DO IT WHY COULDN'T HE?

In today's society, we have to look far and wide for solid examples of what family should look like. With the divorce rate at over 50 percent and broken homes being the norm, it is refreshing to see families intact for a change. Strangely enough, reality television has had two programs over the past few years that put a positive spin on the nuclear family. What made these shows even more interesting was the fact that they were about rappers and their families. People have varying opinions of rap music and rappers. There are those who believe that rap music is nothing but dehumanizing, hate-filled vulgarity, being put out by heartless, hopeless, self-centered, money hungry rappers, who only care about themselves. For many rappers in the music industry these negative characterizations do not accurately depict them. Fortunately, these shows allowed America to see another side of these hip-hop artists. This is not to defend those rappers who actually do fit into those stereotypical roles, however, it goes to show that not all of these artists are as they are portrayed in the media or in videos.

One rapper who has set a very good example of what it means to be a daddy was on a popular reality television show that originally premiered on music television in 2005. The rapper is one of the fore-fathers of hip-hop music and was part of a world-renowned rap group. Most notably, this rapper has given his life over to the Lord and preaches the gospel. The show was about the rapper and his wife raising their six children and dealing with the challenges that many parents face.

One of the things that my family and I liked most about the show was at the end the rapper would send out a positive message to all of his viewers and readers about what he had learned in that episode. His story is truly inspirational because he is a shining example of what GOD can do in a person's life. Being one of the pioneers of rap I'm sure he has tons of stories to tell about touring around the world; having millions of dollars and lots of women throwing themselves at him. The transformation in this rapper is significant especially when considering what his lifestyle must have been like earlier in his career.

Obviously, he had to be apart from his family when he was away on tour. The comparison between how he is now after settling down and his prior lifestyle is probably amazing. In my opinion, the latter story of his life is the greater story. The mature man we saw each week on the show most likely had to grow into his role as a daddy, it did not happen overnight. The love and patience he would exhibit toward his children and the wisdom he presented to the world had to be developed over many years. This rapper's approach toward family was what made the show so entertaining. It was a great example of what fatherhood really means.

If people found it easy to accept that a rapper turned reverend could be a good daddy, others would find it utterly impossible for a gangsta rapper to be a positive role model as a daddy. I'm positive I will receive criticism for using a gangsta rapper as an example of fatherhood. I feel like, who better to demonstrate that all it takes is a commitment and love in order for a man to be a daddy. For me, this gangsta rapper's show really helped to put this book into perspective. The show aired on the Entertainment Television channel in 2007. Ironically enough, the show was about one of the most highly regarded gangsta rappers in the music business.

I'm sure the show was the complete opposite of what most people expected it to be about. Almost everyone in America, both black and white, know this rapper as a hard core hip-hop artist. It is likely that many viewers expected to see this rapper verbally attacking women or dealing with multiple babies mothers. On the contrary, this was a show about a married man who was raising his children along with his wife. The program showed the rapper taking an active role in his children's lives. He was a football coach and sponsored youth football teams, he took his children to his high school even though he didn't graduate. He wanted his children to know the teachers who actually inspired him. This man has even gone so far as to even help to support a child that was not biologically his own.

Yes, this *"hardcore gangsta rapper"* had a show about being a daddy. I began to wonder to myself, how ironic is it that the man who has a song about a murder case being brought against him and another song about being one *of America's Most Wanted,* was a real life daddy and not an uncaring thug. This artist dispelled some of the stereotypes that many people have placed on rappers, especially him. To make the situation even sweeter he was raising his kids along with his wife and not just a girlfriend. Most importantly, he was there, present and accounted for when it came to raising his children. He was not a sideline daddy, he was a player in the game as well as a coach. What a wonderful example of family for people to see.

The other significant thing about these shows for me was they portray black men in a positive light. The shows also help to establish that no matter who you are or what your background, you can endeavor to be a daddy to your children. People may have varying opinions of rappers, but the reality of the situation is that these two men are doing what many men will not.

So I asked myself, what's the difference between men like these rappers and other men who vacate their responsibilities? What I'm saying is, if this *"gangsta"* is willing to raise his children, why aren't other men? Do they think their *"player"* card will be revoked if they do the right thing? Is there concern that other gangsters will think they have lost their edge if they show love or concern for someone else? Are these really the reasons that so many young men are running away from their responsibilities?

Maybe these rappers did not start out at the point that they are today. To be honest, I don't know the back-story for either rapper regarding their relationships with other women or their children's mothers. I'm sure there may have been lots of bumps for both of them along the way. The thing I appreciate about these men and the shows is that they help to elevate the concept of family. More importantly, these shows help to establish that even when society has written someone off as a *"trouble maker"* or a *"thug"* they can still prove the naysayers wrong. These men help demonstrate that being a daddy does not make a man *"soft"* or *"weak"*. In fact, it conveyed the total opposite, it actually helps to establish that it takes a real man, a courageous man, to stay and raise his children.

Thus, the question remains, what is it that prevents so many men from sticking around to take care of their kids? Many of us who have grown up without our daddies would like this question answered. It's obvious that there is no one answer that will address every situation. I'm not claiming to have all of the answers, but I just want to expound on some of the reasons I have heard and observations I have made as to why some men abandon ship. Please keep in mind, the main purpose of this book is to explore the effects that growing up without a daddy can have on their children.

As you read this book keep in mind, there is no one size fits all approach when it comes to how a *daddiless* child will navigate life without their father. Not everyone's situation is identical, some scenarios are more extreme than others. There is no way to predict how a person's past experiences will be manifested whether they are internalized or vocalized. If you are a *daddiless* child who is reading this book or a person who knows someone in this category, I hope this book will provide a relatable perspective that deepens your degree of understanding about the *daddiless* issue, as well as, provide a forum to heal past hurts.

Chapter II.

CONCEPTION AND BIRTH

Not too many of us want to think about the moment that we were conceived. The idea of your mother and father being intimate is not a visual we want to dwell on; however, when we put things into perspective it is from the moment that our mothers and fathers laid down together that our lives were being shaped. The moment of conception begins our journey in life. I believe the circumstances that exist when a child is conceived really matter. For example, if a child is conceived in love, happiness, and marriage, as opposed to lust, rape, shame or desperation, the circumstances can have dramatically different impacts on the child's development and growth. In many instances, these conditions translate into the feelings that parents have toward one another and subsequently their child.

It is undeniable that the whole process of conception is a miracle. All of the required conditions have to be met with laser like precision or conception won't take place. A man's sperm must fight for its position among the millions of sperms surrounding it. The sperm has to be strong enough to swim against the current to reach the ovum while being the first to arrive to gain its reward of being accepted by the egg. The temperature, the area, the relationship between these two organisms must be exact. If one element is out of balance, there won't be a baby. Isn't GOD awesome in how he designed the conception process? It is absolutely amazing how many people take this miracle for granted.

Is it true that once in the womb the fetus begins to experience the emotions or feelings its mother encounters? According to medical facts, this is a proven phenomenon. For example, it has been established that ingesting drugs like crack cocaine or smoking cigarettes during pregnancy can have detrimental effects on the growth and physiology of a baby before as well as after birth. Therefore, it stands to reason that if a mother is scared, angry, or even happy, their child could be a mirror image reflecting the emotions of their mother before, during and after birth.

There may be varying opinions regarding when and if a fetus can perceive emotions, nonetheless a journey undeniably begins at the moment of conception. This being the case, it should not be hard to imagine that during this time if the mother is happy this will quite possibly have a positive effect on the baby. To take this point one step further, if a mother takes care of herself while pregnant then her baby will benefit from her diligence. For example, if the mother-to-be eats healthy, feels good about herself and the fact that she is carrying her baby, this may improve the chances of the child being born at the proper birth weight with fewer complications. There are exceptions to the outcome described above; however, a content and conscientious mother will lead to a happy healthy baby in many instances.

Let's contrast the prior scenario with that of an expectant mother who concealed her pregnancy from her family because she became pregnant by a young man during a one-night stand. The situation is exacerbated because she does not know his name or anything about him. She fears that if her parents find out about her circumstance they will throw her out of the house. What are the potential consequences for the unborn child in this situation? The young woman's clothes are too tight as she is attempting to squeeze into her pre-pregnancy clothes even though her mid-section is ever expanding; and this is possibly affecting the baby's growth. She continues to eat junk food and is irresponsible with her diet. Required doctor visits are neglected while she foregoes necessary checkups that help to ensure the child is developing properly. Compounding all of this is the fact that the girl may not want the child. She feels guilty, scared, frustrated, confused, and angry with herself for having sex without using a condom. She is also angry with the boy for being so irresponsible and getting her pregnant. Unfortunately, these are the situations we hear about on the news, the tragic tails of children being born outside of a hospital in a high school bathroom or worse.

Even if the young woman happens to know the identity of the baby's father it does not always mean the situation is going to be positive. Many times the two of them will constantly argue in her attempts to convince him to take care of his obligations or over his suggestions to *"get rid of the problem"* by having an abortion. Some of the aforementioned situations are extreme; however, they do occur. Walking among us every day are children who were born on the floors of schoolhouse bathrooms, wrapped in jackets with the umbilical cord and placenta still attached, or wrapped in newspapers and discarded in trash heaps like garbage. It is unimaginable the extreme loneliness that this mother and her child must feel in this situation. There is no telling what the long-term effects of being born in these environments will have on the children or their mothers for that matter.

In stark contrast, consider a baby being born in a cozy hospital with doctors and nurses there to address any possible complications. There are support personnel present to explain to the mother what is happening, how she can assist in the delivery of the baby, as well as, someone there to hold her hand and tell her everything will be all right. Once the child is delivered, the airways and mouth are suctioned, the umbilical cord is cut, the baby is put under a heat lamp, swaddled, and given to the mother for feeding. This baby is welcomed into a warm, safe, loving environment where, at minimum, the child is cared for, wanted and possibly even loved. This ideal situation would include the father of the child being present to hold, nurture and assist in the care of the newborn. With the father's presence may come acceptance and love versus rejection and emptiness for both the mother and her child.

Picture the child opening its eyes, blinking to focus after completing the long tumultuous journey through the birth canal. After enduring the physical pain of the contractions beating against its body, the child is then exposed to unfamiliar sounds and feeling. Entry into this strange world where it is cold, big and full of people who are all unfamiliar, leaves the child traumatized. The trauma of such an occurrence would be hard for any adult to comprehend and survive, let alone a newborn. So even after surviving the difficulty of childbirth, the child still has to deal with the fact that his or her birth was the result of an unwanted pregnancy. This situation has *motive* or *motivation* written all over it.

Granted, not all situations where the father is present for the birth of his child will be pleasant and loving. Sometimes even if he is there, it is not predetermined whether his influence will be a *motive* or a *motivation* situation. There are circumstances where even if a father is physically present he is not an active participant in his child's life. I will discuss these dysfunctional situations later in this book; however, the overall point to be made here is that the beginning of *motive or motivation* journey begins on day one.

Chapter III.
MOMMA'S BABY DADDY'S MAYBE

How can you ignore your child? How can you deny their existence and not make them a part of your life? Isn't there a hunger, a calling, a force pulling at your heart that makes you want to know whether your offspring is all right and taken care of? It is amazing that these questions even need to be posed at all. I understand there are some situations where a father may not be aware that he has a child or that the child's mother was even pregnant. Maybe she became pregnant during a one-night stand or an uncommitted short-term relationship. Even when the pregnancy occurs with two people who have been in a monogamous relationship, his first instinct may be to deny that the child is his. It has become commonplace for men to first deny being a child's father and force the mother to obtain a DNA test before they are willing to acknowledge their child. Obviously, erring on the side of caution is the rational, but in many of these situations this is simply an avoidance method. The issue of men denying their children has been a problem throughout history. My philosophy for any guy who want to have sex is *"if you lay down as a boy you better be ready to stand up as a man."*

THE GHETTO DNA TEST

My first meeting with my father was awkward to say the least. Here I was a thirteen-year-old boy who had decided a few weeks earlier that I wanted to meet the man that was partially responsible for my existence. As he entered our apartment with his cousin, it was strange because I initially did not know which man was my father. I scanned them both up and down when they walked in the door. They looked me up and down as well. I guessed we were all trying to decide if there was any resemblance. Then my mother made the big announcement, "This is Frank", that's my father's name. In my thirteen years, we had never laid eyes on one another. I had not even seen a picture of the man, so I could have walked right by him on the street without even realizing it. So there we stood in this awkward moment. Then my father's cousin stated, *"Man he's got the same ears as Raphael."* I later learned that Raphael was my half-brother. I presumed my ears were the distinguishing feature we had been looking for to establish that we were father and son.

Years later when I became an adult I asked Frank if he wanted to take a paternity test to make it official; he said he didn't need it because he knew I was his son. I was not sure if the examination was enough, but apparently it was enough for him. My mother had always told me that Frank was my father and I guess he knew it too.

The question that I pose from this story is how many times has this episode been played out, this ghetto paternity test? The mother is there at the hospital or at home and the boy or man enters with one of his family members or even a friend. The child is examined, better yet scrutinized, to find some identifiable likeness between the two of them. I guess it is not so bad for the child when they are very young, but in a situation like mine you can just imagine how that can make a person feel.

Personally, I felt empty, somewhat bitter and angry. I felt as if I was being evaluated like a piece of cattle to determine whether I passed inspection. It seems that in these situations there has to be a seal of approval from a grandmother, an aunt, an uncle or even a friend regarding the paternity of a child. Statements may be made such as, *"Oh look, he has your forehead, or she has your eyes, nose, ears, cheeks, or mouth"* thereby confirming fatherhood.

It is ironic how this same first meeting can be so different at times. The meeting can unfold in a more loving, and endearing manner when it occurs with a married couple who has no doubt about their child's paternity. This type of introduction is more often comprised of loving comparisons of features instead of an uncomfortable examination.

But what about those scenarios where there are no outward or obvious features that prove paternity? Consider the times when the child is paraded in front of "grandma" and she declares, *"that child looks nothing like him!"* These are the types of denials that can either create *motives* or provide *motivation*. As these young children grow up someone in their family may have the daunting task of explaining that their father denied them. Even if the father later attains a deeper level of maturity and wants to have a relationship with his child, the desire to reconnect may not be mutual. How damaging can it potentially be to a child to have their paternity question answered in public?

This scenario plays out almost daily when mothers appear on the *"You Are Not The Father Show"*. Clearly, I have changed the title here in order to emphasize my point, but the scenarios generally develop the same way. Women initially arrive on the show very boastful and certain, making claims that one individual or another is the father of their child. These mothers tend to appear visibly shocked to hear the host of the show say, *"The results are in and you are not the father"*. It is as if they did not pay attention to the title of the show. Given the name of the show it would seem obvious that the man they brought on the show would not be the father. The humiliating part about this is the child will have access to see the alleged fathers act a fool while their mother's are being made to look like tramps as the man calls her *"ho, slut"* and other demeaning names. After an episode like that it's no wonder that the child may feel like an unwanted bastard that only a mother could love. What makes the *"You Are Not The Father Show"* scenario more shameful is the fact that the entire spectacle is memorialized on tape for the child as well as the rest of the world to see. An individual observing this would have to be in a state of denial to think that an experience like this would not be a possible *motive* for that child.

On the other hand, the reality is that some women may be too embarrassed to seek a DNA test for fear of being stereotyped and perceived by others as being promiscuous. She is concerned that people will think, *"that girl was so loose she does not even know who the father of her child is."* Many of these women view the test as a confirmation of their immorality as opposed to a method to confirm paternity.

Ironically, in these instances the mothers cannot deny that the children are theirs. The father can deny the child until the day the paternity test results are obtained or until the day he dies, the same is not true for the mothers. In the hood there has always been an old saying *"mama's baby daddy's maybe"*.

Unfortunately, being denied by your father has become an almost natural and common response to assertions of fathering a child.

Being rejected or denied in any way is hard for any man, woman, boy or girl, but to be denied by a person that is supposed to be one of the most significant people in your life, well that takes on a whole different degree of pain. In many cases, the feelings are either internalized and bottled up for years or manifested in a variety of positive and negative ways. This rejection can lead to abandonment issues and constant feelings of not being accepted throughout their lives. However, most of all the denial by a father can definitely serve as a *"motive"* or *"motivation"*.

Chapter IV.

GENERATIONAL CURSE

On Friday, April 11, 2008, my wife and I along with another couple we know from Atlanta, Georgia were at our home watching an interesting documentary called *"Meeting David Wilson"*. The program was about an African-American man who searched historical records and located the descendants of the white family who once enslaved his ancestors. The story was intriguing because it documented a first meeting between two people who did not know one another but were eternally connected. The meeting was significant because the man was able to obtain answers to many of the questions he had relating to how his ancestors lived, their history, and his lineage.

In many ways, *daddiless* children can relate to this man's plight. Most of us *daddiless* children go through our lives at a disadvantage because we do not have that essential information that this man was able to obtain. Many times, we go through our lives asking questions such as where are my ancestors from because we grow up not knowing our own family's history. Do they have a history of mental or physical health issues? Are there talented people that may be a part of my family tree?

We have no idea who our relatives might be because we have no point of reference as to who they are. In many ways; we feel and we are disconnected, by not being associated with all sides of our lives. There is essentially an entire side of us that seems like it is missing and there is a sense that we are not a whole person. How do you function when a part of you is not there? It can be compared to having lost an arm or a leg. For many healthy people, not saying we aren't, who have always had that part of their body, there would be a great sense of loss to lose one of these important parts. They have an opportunity to use that part of them every day so if it is suddenly taken away there is a real readjustment period. For some they never adjust and for others they learn to get along just fine without it. Yeah, they may be looked at funny or even talked about, but overall they grin and bear it. This is analogous to a situation where a child has lost their father due to divorce or has had some time to be with him and he leaves.

There is another aspect to this as well. If you're an African-American, these feelings are amplified many times over because we are the descendants of people who were stolen from their native land. As a community at large we do not know our ancestry, this fact compounds the disadvantage we have in comparison to our *daddiless* counterparts of other ethnic backgrounds.

So first, there is a feeling of being disconnected from our ancestors like the man in the documentary was, but then the feelings are heightened by being left *daddiless*. We're disconnected on two distinct levels. Attempting to trace one's distant history will be an exercise in futility unless the immediate family history is known.

In addition to feeling cut off, there is the fact that most children will emulate the things they see growing up. Some fathers will repeat events they experienced whether consciously or subconsciously. Whether they were abandoned, abused, or even treated well, these actions are repeated generation after generation. In some families, the issue of *daddilessness* has been prevalent for many years. The *daddiless* problem can be linked with alcoholism, drug abuse, and in some cases physical and mental abuse. These are unhealthy attributes passed down from one generation to the next like family heirlooms. I consider these re-manifestations generational curses.

Many times, the issues that brought about the curse in the first place have been kept a secret for so long that there may not be any way of knowing when it originated. The thing that has lived on in these curses is the pain that they have caused. This pain can result in fathers not knowing how to deal with and address the issue of having a child. The cycles of physical and mental abuse may also lead to dysfunctional relationships between a child's mother and father that may result in abandonment by the man. Further, if a boy grew up without his father he may very well lack the know-how to be a father. Thus, he may not be willing to explore parenthood himself and unfortunately this may carry on the *daddiless* legacy.

Breaking these family curses is one of the greatest acts a *daddiless* child can achieve. The question becomes, how does one break these curses? Some of these plagues are the results of suffering that has been observed for many years. Without positive examples, these individuals don't realize there are alternatives to their current way of life. In order to begin the process of change it will require a different mindset that will involve different relationships and a great deal of self-determination.

It will be important to look at the environment and the people that are around you. If these surroundings or individuals are not adding any value to the life that you want then they need to be removed or changed. These changes will require looking beyond the negative things that have become the norm and turning to individuals for guidance that have proven themselves responsible. It is important that alternative behaviors be identified that will promote a promising outlook on life. Seek out family members or friends who have been successful in overcoming obstacles.

A lot of times family or friends can expose those secrets that have bound up the family for so long. Talking about those things that have caused so much pain will most likely generate positive results. Releasing those dark demons that have smothered optimism, hope, and trust will provide you with peace and perspective. There will be peace because you have an awareness of what it is that plagues you. There is perspective because you realize that there is pain associated with the reasoning of the person who has caused the curse to be perpetuated. Whether you're on the giving or receiving end of this information really does not matter, what is important is you have a better understanding of how the curse began so you know what to do to avoid it occurring again. Thus, with an understanding of the past you will create hope for the future.

It is also very important to know that change may not come instantaneously. There may not be an immediately identifiable thing that you can put your finger on and say the curse is over. However, it is important not to get discouraged because things are not happening as quickly as you like. Just know that the changes that you make today will pay dividends in your life tomorrow. I encourage you to associate yourself with individuals who have established their ability to raise healthy families and achieve other goals in their lives. It is also important to begin exploring new environments and new people. Expand your horizons by going to new places outside of where you live. Go about meeting new people and seek out new experiences. Once these individuals and places have been identified, begin to use them as the positive examples that you need to break your own generational curses.

Just being *daddiless* can be a *"motivation"* by itself because most *daddiless* children desire change. The desire to break generational curse and potentially be better parents may be one of the best ways to end these long lasting cycles. The desire to experience a better way of life for yourself and for your children can be one of the greatest influences for change. Thus, the best way to break the *daddiless* curses and cycles is a desire for change and actions that move you in that direction. When you don't have examples, you should become one.

Chapter V.

FINANCIAL SUPPORT

Many times *daddiless* children are mocked and made fun of for being the *"bastard"* child of some unknown man. In many cases, we're also made fun of because of the financial situations that are created when our fathers aren't there.

I remember how it was for me growing up in the ghettos of Columbus, Ohio. Poindexter Village was a subsidized housing project primarily for mothers on welfare. In this project, few families had two parents in the household. If the father was in the home he was probably not well-educated, may have been an alcoholic, a drug addict or either he could not afford to provide for the number of children who lived with him. As with anything, there are exceptions to the rule, but these were the situations in the projects where I lived. Interestingly enough, in the majority of circumstances the man or father was not even supposed to be in the household because it was presumed that if he was present the family must have been over the income limit to live there. Thus, whenever management conducted inspections of the apartments any men in the households would vacate the premises at least temporarily.

The income determinations are a little different today and there is more of a focus on keeping the family unit together, however, when I was growing up a mother had to be on her own in order to qualify for subsidized housing or financial assistance. It's fascinating, there was and still is an expectation that if there is a man in a household he should be able to afford everything associated with his family. Regardless of how educated or how much money he actually earns the expectation still exists. The man is supposed to be the breadwinner, the provider, no matter what the situation involves. Being a man, I can now appreciate how much responsibility is placed upon us just because we are men. I recognize how much of an impact that I have on my family and our way of life. Knowing that my family is depending on me I realize and accept this responsibility. I welcome the responsibility because it makes me better.

I reflect on how our financial difficulties affected me growing up. For one, we lived in the projects, which automatically revealed we were poor. I recall the utter embarrassment I felt when I went to the corner store or the supermarket with food stamps. I really hated going to the store with food stamps with a passion. The welfare system was not as it is today with the smart card that looks like and is used similarly to a debit card. Back in those days, we had paper food stamps. These food coupons could be used like cash. The only problem was food stamps could only be used to buy food and nothing else. Any toiletries or other items had to be purchased with actual cash.

I remember very vividly the times my mother would send me to the store to buy her cigarettes. To this day I still remember her brand, Benson & Hedges Menthol in the green pack. I would always lobby for my brothers to go to the store instead of me. Sadly, I was the youngest and my protests usually were made in vain. At that time, there were no age restrictions on buying a pack of cigarettes, even a four or five year old could have made the purchase.

However, being sent to the store was not the real issue. The thing that I despised the most was the fact that I was sent to the store with food stamps. The issue was compounded even further in that I was to use food stamps to buy items that were not food. Cigarettes do not fall into the category of edible items like food, thus in order to buy the cigarettes I had to change food stamps into coins to make the purchase. Cigarettes cost about a dollar fifty a pack at that time. The transaction was completely humiliating because I first had to purchase an inexpensive item like a pack of *"Now and Laters"* candy for about a dime; thereby, breaking one of the one dollar food stamps. I received the change from the first transaction and then repeated the purchase to break another dollar food stamp to have enough for the cigarettes. I ended up with about a dollar and eighty cents for those of you who were keeping count. This generally required that I make at least three transactions, two to break the first two food stamps and the last one to buy the cigarettes. If you asked for the second pack of *"Now and Laters"* before the cashier gave you the change then it would be taken out of the first dollar, thus you would not have enough money to buy the cigarettes so timing was important. This was a delicate transaction for a kid but I did it repeatedly.

I ducked and dodged to avoid being seen by my friends spending food stamps. Furthermore, when I made these purchases I never wanted to go to the store with my friends because I did not want to them to know my family was on welfare, even though most of my friend's families were on welfare too. Just think about it, they lived in the same projects as I did; however, at the time I didn't make the connection between living in the projects and being on welfare. There was a positive side to the whole transaction for me as a kid, I got two packs of *"Now and Laters"* for my trouble. Sometimes I was allowed to keep the other thirty cents that was left over too, but that was beside the point. I was still embarrassed.

Another side affect of our financial situation was our clothing. I remember going with my mother and brothers to an organization called *"Charity Newsie."* Now that I look back on the program it was a wonderful philanthropic organization, but at the time, I looked at it as if it were the plague. *"Charity Newsie"* was a program that provided clothes and assistance for children from low-income families. The program would provide two pairs of blue jeans, a pack of underwear, a pack of t-shirts, a pack of socks, a winter coat (most of the time it was made of wool so it was extremely itchy, but warm), and a voucher for a pair of shoes from *"Payless."* Yes, I said "Payless". We called the shoes *"Buddies"* or *"BoBo"* because none of them had a designer name or logo. The voucher would not buy any designer shoes.

The clothes from *"Charity Newsie"* were also very identifiable and distinct. For example, the design on the pocket of the jeans was a stitched circle; the coat was similar to a wool lumberjack shirt with big red and black checkers, it was heavy and rather ugly. Due to the very distinguished look of these clothes, most of my friends knew that we went to the "Newsie" to get our clothes. Therefore, when my brothers and I went to school you can imagine how we felt when kids would tease us about where we had gotten our clothes. In an effort to reduce our embarrassment, we would not wear our coats even though it was the middle of winter. As for the jeans, we would use a pair of scissors to remove the circle stitching from the pockets of the pants to make people think we were wearing *"plain pockets"*. In the 1980s Levi's *"Plain Pocket jeans"* were in style, so we cut the stitching from the pants pockets and we thought people would think we were wearing the latest fashion. The only thing was our jeans did not have the trademark orange Levi's tag that proved that the jeans were authentic. Therefore, when somebody was wearing a pair of real Levi's they would call us out on it. During this time, we would either fight or attempt to make fun of the other person by playing the dozens in order to avoid being embarrassed. If a kid was not witty or couldn't think fast on their feet, they would probably get angry then start a fight to put a halt to the teasing. Many of us *daddiless* kids did not like the dozens very much because once another kid talked about us not having a daddy it would result in a fistfight soon thereafter.

In 1997, one of my favorite rappers described his experience growing up without having many clothes. In his rap he spoke about only having two pairs of jeans and sewing designer tags on his shirts in order to make it look like he had the expensive clothes he saw other kids wearing. When someone would point out that his clothes were fakes he said he would punch them in the face. The words he spoke rang very true for kids growing up the way we did. This type of response was typical in the our neighborhood whenever someone felt disrespected.

In many cases, feelings of humiliation and shame can be influenced or amplified when a child's father is absent. The lack of a father's financial support can push a child in a variety of directions sometimes to theft and desperation. The reality is that people will resort to some very drastic measures when they are hungry or when they desire to have what they see others with. On the other hand there are those who look internally for fortitude, their strong will to succeed and have a better life helps them to establish a stronger work ethic and a desire to change their financial situations through legal means.

The child's perspective on how desperate their financial situation is can play a pivotal role in their decision-making, but under the surface, there will always be an underlying blame of their father for their financial woes. Statements like *"he should have been here to take care of his responsibilities"* or *"he ain't no man because a real man wouldn't have left his kids like this"* are all common phrases. This blame or distain for these fathers may be even greater if he in fact lived in better circumstances then his child. The child tends to believe that their life could have been like his or better had he been there. So in the child's mind their father allowed them to suffer while he lived the good life.

Not having a daddy present to inspire strong values or to provide potential relief to the financial situation may ultimately produce positive or negative decision-making. The standpoint from which the child views their *daddiless* situation can make or break the child's spirit. These perceptions can make children; hard and cold; weak or strong; even bold and courageous. For those who use their *daddilessness* as a *motive* it can result in them believing that their callousness or lack of caring is what makes them courageous and strong. In many instances they are afraid to show any emotions or let anyone into their hearts because they were hurt so badly by their past. Many of these individuals avoid lasting relationships and commitment because they don't want to feel that hurt again. The perceived consequences of their *daddilessness* become their cause, their reason for continuing to be heartless. This is the most unfortunate result of them all because in many cases it can lead to self-destructive behavior.

One final point on the topic of financial support. It is important for those fathers who are present in their children's lives to recognize that being a good provider financially does not equate to being a good daddy. There are always those children who have their fathers around for financial support but he is completely absent when it comes to their emotional needs. These children may go down the wrong path just as fast as those whose father is absent.

When it comes to *daddiless* children, what's important about the issue of financial support or the lack thereof is, even though it is an uncomfortable position to be in when you do not have your needs met, a positive outcome can still come about. Strength can be gained and character developed when one is forced to go without. Even being mocked or ridiculed can still create the push that will make a person stronger. Sometimes when we are deprived of something, it teaches us valuable lessons about the difference between wants and needs. Integrity is built and demonstrated in how we react when we must have or desire something. For example, do you go out and work for food when you're hungry or do you resort to stealing from day to day to eat? Do you employ a short-term solution to resolve a long-term problem? Do you figure out a way to find a job or obtain your education, so that you can provide necessities for the duration? These questions need to be answered before one can turn a potential *motive* into *motivation*.

Chapter VI.

THE MOTIVE

Remember earlier when I said that growing up without a father is like having lost an important body part? I compared it to losing an arm or a leg. Well, most of us can understand this comparison because we use our arms and legs every day. The same principle applies to our parents because we need and use them daily for many different reasons. Living without one of these parental limbs can have a devastating effect on a person's life. Furthermore, in some cases, being raised without a father is like growing up without a heart. Some young men and women develop and don't really care about anyone or anything. The rationale is that his or her father didn't have the heart to stick around, so this child doesn't have a heart to care for anyone else.

Many things such as; broken relationships, multiple partners, no feelings of commitment, a lack of stability, and no dedication, can all be *motives* for heartless behaviors. The results of damaging associations can lead to a child going through life aimlessly looking for a missing puzzle piece. That puzzle piece for thousands, maybe millions, of *daddiless* children is their absent father.

In some cases, the mother becoming pregnant was *motive* enough for the father to leave, but in others cases the *motives* are different. So what were his? Was he married? Was it just a one-night stand? Was there a divorce? Was he sent to prison? On the other hand, was he just continuing the generational curse, the cycle of *daddilessness* that he experienced growing up? Some of the most unfortunate situations are those where the father says he was not around because he did not want to pay child support. Child support. Nevertheless, a desire to avoid paying child support is a real *"motive"* for some men.

Child Support as a "motive"

People are willing to lie, cheat, steal, and sell their babies for money. There is a significant financial cost associated with having a child; sometimes it takes a court order before some men are willing to pay these costs. In many states, a failure to pay support will result in wage garnishment, followed by jail time if the person refuses to pay for an extended period. I recall a case in the news where a professional football player conspired to have his girlfriend murdered after she informed him of her pregnancy. It was asserted by the prosecution in the case that the primary reason the player arranged the girlfriends murder was because he did not want to pay child support. Unfortunately, the mother died of her gunshot wounds. In a twist of fate, the unborn child lived which meant the main objective of the plot was thwarted.

Here was a man earning millions of dollars as a professional athlete, however, he was willing to go to the extreme of taking another person's life just to avoid paying money. In hindsight, I'm sure he regrets the decision, especially considering the fact that the amount of support he was trying to avoid would have been significantly less than what he actually lost financially and otherwise. Now he has nothing except a jail cell to look at every day and the money that he earned is pretty much useless. He may be able to receive a little more (than other inmates) from the commissary, but the luxuries that he had become accustomed to are all gone. How ridiculously ironic was this decision? His long-term solution to a short-term situation was to kill. Now, his actual *motive*, to hoard his money, has no real value. A pack of cigarettes or a Little Debbie snack cake is probably worth more than actual currency to him, now that he's in jail. All of this was done in an effort to avoid making monthly child support payments. Does this make logical sense in the grand scheme of things? I would say not.

Child support is a big deal to some men because they expect to maintain a certain lifestyle; adding a child to the equation becomes just another financial obligation. What is overlooked when a child's life is reduced to a financial duty is that this child is a human being, a person. It is truly unexplainable how some people are willing to put such minuscule value on a human life. However, worse than the avoidance of the financial responsibility, the child has to live without the companionship of his or her father because of money. How absurd is that? A person is going to allow a few dollars to be the thing that will come between him and his own flesh and blood. Many men have the attitude that they should not have to pay for something they did not want in the first place.

How selfish can a person be? In many instances, the issue of child support highlights this question. We know all too well that the disturbing answer to this question is that people can be unimaginably selfish, some more than others. When a man is asked to pay the costs associated with having a child, you get an opportunity to see up close and personally how self-centered he can really be. When the mother and father separate child support can be the *motive* for even some of the most loving parents to disappear. In various cases, the issue of money can create a huge split in priorities along with a denial of responsibility.

Today the phrase *"dead beat dads"* refers to men that have been court ordered to pay child support but have failed to meet their financial obligations. These men have accumulated enormous arrearages due to their failures to pay. There are various reasons as to why they have accumulated large child support debts. Some do not have jobs or have even quit jobs in order to avoid paying their support. Others work jobs and do not report their income, or they report part of it in order to get a reduction in their support payment. Our current economy has also negatively influenced some men's ability to pay because many of them have been laid off. Job or no job, the support payments still continue to amass and must be paid.

Most of these men know that delinquent child support can lead to incarceration, as well as a felony record. It is also understood that failure to pay child support can lead to the loss of licenses as well. Some men who are licensed professionals have lost their licenses to practice medicine, law, and even their driver's licenses, for not paying child support. Stripping a man of his license or sending him to jail does not seem to be the best option to address the issue of not paying. To be honest, it seems like it would make the situation worse because the mother may never receive the outstanding funds if the man's means of earning money is taken away. Thus, the cycle continues. While I understand that there has to be some consequence for these *"deadbeat dads"*, I question if this is the best way to get the point across.

Alternatively, there are men who actually pay the support, but do not want anything to do with the child. Again, it seems that a dollar value is being placed on the child's life. The child is viewed as a *"bill"* or a *"payment"* instead of an actual human being with feelings. There is a cost associated with these situations; however, it is not financial and most likely will not be paid by the father. The price that tends to be paid will be borne to the child in the form of emotional burdens that go along with being devalued by his or her father. Society pays the cost in many instances, depending on how the child deals with his or her circumstances. The community at large may pay in the form of incarceration costs, welfare, and public assistance programs.

It seems at times that some fathers have more concern for their *"property"* than they do for their own flesh and blood. This lack of concern can result in children growing up broken and feeling diminished. More than that, why don't these men look at the effect rejection has on the minds and spirits of their children? It's as if these fathers have subconsciously reduced their children down to inanimate objects. Once the child is devalued as less than human it is easier for their fathers to live with themselves. This mind-set is similar to that of slave owners during slavery; reduce people to less than human and you can treat them worse than animals. It may be the remnants of slavery that causes some African-American men to continue in the same manner when dealing with their children.

Is it possibly easier for a man to live with himself if he does not think about his child as a human and more like a possession without feelings? I hope that fathers and mothers who feel this way about their children realize that what goes around comes around.

Looking at my own experience, the issue of child support brings up thoughts of what could have been. My mother never asked my father for any support. In fact, she did not ask for support from my brother's father either. I really do not know why she never asked for money or even pursued a paternity test for any of us. The paternity test would have at least established the identity of our fathers. Maybe she was too proud, maybe she did not know the process, nonetheless it did not happen. Therefore, we grew up on welfare and food stamps in some of the worst neighborhoods in the city of Columbus, Ohio. Today, the situation would probably be different because the welfare department now requires mothers to pursue child support or they will not receive benefits.

More than anything, I wonder how my life might have unfolded, if at least one of our fathers had paid support or if all of them had contributed. I would not have minded being viewed as a bill or a payment if it would have helped us escape the ghetto. A single mother trying to raise three boys on her own, without a high school diploma is a considerable feat; we were destined for rough times. Had our fathers been asked to pay child support, would we have lived in the projects? Would we have endured days when we were hungry? Would we have had to wear clothes from charity? None of these questions will ever be answered, but we can always wonder.

I feel compelled to ask, would more fathers be active in their children's lives if the child support obligations were not present? I am sure there are some men that would be willing to be involved with their children if they were not forced to pay child support. Overall, is that really a good reason to abandon your child? I do not think so and most *daddiless* children would agree. If a man is that self-centered and money hungry then maybe the child is better off without him in their life anyway.

Prison as a "motive"

The penitentiary has been a major contributing factor in children being *daddiless* in the United States. Incarceration is prevalent in minority communities, especially the African American and Hispanic populations. It has become a commonplace occurrence for young children to know that their father is serving time in prison and will not be coming home for an extended period. Many men have argued that their *motive* for committing crimes was their family. Their claims are that crime was the only means they had to feed their children. I presume if these men did not get caught committing these crimes it could have been a short-term means of caring for them. The reality of the situation is that once these individuals are caught and convicted, they will not be able to provide for those they claim to care for, especially from behind bars. So the question is, what good did committing the crime really do for him or his family?

I am a firm believer in doing what is necessary to take care of your off spring, but I also believe in making appropriate choices. The decisions that I made early in my life helped to determine the options I had available to me later in life. I know each situation is different and there are extreme cases where a person has only been exposed to a life of crime. They were taught at early ages that the only way to survive was to commit crimes or perish. I know there are people in this world who really believe that this philosophy is true; I actually grew up with some of them. On the other hand, there are men and women who want the fast money and the fast lifestyle. In our "*right now generation*", people are not willing to wait to achieve their goals. There are those who live by the creed, "*why would I make five hundred dollars every two weeks when I can make five thousand dollars a day?*" The question, "*What will this quick money cost me,"* is only an echo for a child who has grown up without their needs being met.

On the contrary, most people believe as I do, freedom is priceless. A free man can achieve more and provide for his family as opposed to being locked up during any part of his child's life. Realistically, there is a very slim chance that a father who is locked up will have an opportunity to impart direct guidance, structure, love and affection to his son or daughter from a jail cell. Moreover, if the father does a long stretch of time in jail and re-enters his child's life, it is extremely difficult for the child to acknowledge his father's role in his life. In these cases, bonds have been broken, or never existed in the first place, and respect has been lost because many of the children have difficulties with taking advice or guidance from an ex-convict. Besides that, many children have the attitude that their father could not possibly know enough about them to provide them with instruction or advice. After all, because they have had to grow-up without him for so many years, they develop a mentality that his efforts are "too little, too late". The unfortunate part about some of these situations is that the father's criminal behavior was the "standout" example that was provided to his child.

Another disastrous consequence of these fathers' decisions is that many of these children will follow the examples set by one of the most influential people in their lives, their parent. A number of these children will follow in their father's footsteps and become criminals themselves. The absence of a positive role model can lead children to follow the only example they've known, that of a criminal. Moreover, even if a father leaves jail with a new outlook on life, his children may still find it extremely difficult to accept advice from someone who is practically a stranger to them. These children are more likely to reject the recommendations of their fathers just because he's the source of the advice. Many of them do not want to take advice from the convicts who left them when they were younger. How could this person come back after all these years and try to impart wisdom? Where was all of that wisdom when the child really needed it?

What's unfortunate is the fact that some of the recommendations from these fathers are actually sound. However, due to the father being the source of this wisdom, the advice may still fall on deaf ears. Regrettably, even when these fathers try and impart wisdom to their children, explaining the consequences of their actions (dropping out of school, etc.), these gestures are still met with skepticism or mistrust because of the lack of a relationship. The advice could be valid or legitimate, however since he's the source it causes the child to push back. It may take years before some of these children will acknowledge that the advice they were given was actually sound, but this is one of the consequences of these strained relationships.

In my opinion, this criminal *motive* can be even more destructive to the relationship between fathers and their children when the father is a habitual criminal. In most cases, he will float in and out of his child's life attempting to be daddy in between jailhouse bids. I witnessed first-hand the amount of resentment that this situation can create. My middle brother's repeated incarcerations were a source of anger and bitterness for his four children. Once my brother was released from prison, he had a great deal of difficulty reconnecting with my nephews and nieces. His relationship with his youngest son was particularly strained by his absence. My brother's drug use and numerous prison stints resulted in his son lacking respect for him and his advice.

One of the main subjects that would cause problems between the two of them was the issue of discipline. My nephew would question my brother's right to discipline him, especially since he had not been there for most of his life. How could someone who had been living outside of the rules for so long now try to have someone abide by his rules? Despite what my nephew went through growing up, he has become a well-mannered, respectful young man, who was able to use his father's missteps in life as a *"motivation"*. He has never been in trouble with the law, has not had children out of wedlock, and continues to pursue his college career. I am extremely proud that this young man looks up to me as his role model. He has not continued the generational curses that have been perpetuated by his father. There is no doubt that my nephew loves his father very much, but the mistakes of the past continue to haunt them both to this day.

    I hope the children of these ex-convicts will be able to look beyond their fathers' mistakes and not emulate them. Most of the fathers of these children do not want their children to follow their example. I would recommend that these children take heed to the words of caution from their fathers. Even if the child despises the man, it is important to understand that he has lived through the negative consequences that bad decisions can bring. If he is telling you not to do what he did, you should listen. I admire my nephew for his ability to avoid the pitfalls that his father did not. I am sure he's a better person just because he was willing to listen, not just to me, but also to the unspoken and spoken lessons that his father's incarceration taught him. He is living proof that a father's incarceration can be a *motivation* for some children and not just a *motive*.

The point overall is that it is asinine for a father to use a criminal enterprise in order to provide for his family. The decisions to use crime as a means to an end can subsequently cost a father all he claims he wants to preserve. Some people may think that crime pays, but in the long-run it can end up costing you the people you claim to love. It is truly amazing what a little or, in some cases, a lot of patience will do. Taking your time to savor the journey will only make it that much sweeter. However, if the journey leads you to prison then it was just a waste. The time that you lose while incarcerated is time with your child that you will never be able to recover. In addition, if you are any type of businessman you know that *"time is money."* However, more than that, the time you will lose with your child can possibly cause him or her to be morally bankrupt and there is no value that you can place on that.

I hope these words will help some men to recognize that they should not allow their *motivation* of caring for their family to become a *motive* to commit crime. If the justification for committing a crime is to take care for your family, just know that this *motivation* may end up turning into a *"motive"* for your children. Despite all of his best intentions if a father believes that crime will produce a positive long-term outcome for his family, he is truly mistaken.

An Affair as a "motive"

There is no one force on the face of the earth, except maybe death, that is more destructive or damaging to a marriage than an affair. Actually, the only other thing that is more catastrophic to a marriage than an affair is a child that is the result of that affair. Imagine, for a moment, being the spouse of someone who comes home one day and says, "I have been involved with someone else". Now, take this scenario a step further and envision being told that in addition to having the affair there was a child conceived. The impact to the spouse on the receiving end of this information can be crushing.

It is not hard to visualize the effect that this situation will have on the adulterer's family, but the impact is deeper than just that family; consider the child born to this circumstance. Here, we have a child that is conceived because of a secret love affair based upon lies, deceit and infidelity. The result in many cases is a child who is left *"daddiless"* because his or her father is married to someone that is not their mother. The secrets continue as the child grows older and begins to wonder where daddy is. The deception also runs very deep because the father is lying to both his wife and his other lover. In many circumstances, this man never intends to leave his wife, but continues to profess his unhappiness in his marriage to his mistress. At the same time, he continues his life with his wife as if nothing has changed. When the other woman becomes pregnant, she's left feeling empty and alone. The mistress winds up in love with a man she may not ever have as her own husband. Moreover, she ends up raising their child by herself.

In many instances the adulterous father continues to sneak around attempting to split his time between the two women and the children. For some women the back and forth gets old after a while and may lead to the infidelity being exposed. The disclosure may come about in some very vindictive ways. For example, imagine being a wife who goes out to the mailbox one day and finding an envelope from the Child Support Enforcement Agency with her husband's name on it. There are not too many wives out there who would not question why their husband is receiving mail from the Child Support Agency. It becomes clear that in certain cases this action is taken in an effort to get back at him for playing both sides of the fence, so to speak. The child may be many years old, even a teenager when this occurs. In her mind this is when the breaking point happens and she cannot tolerate his lies any longer. The truth of the matter may be that the documents are sent when his mistress feels neglected or deceived by *"her man"* because of too many broken promises. Many of these women tend to perceive the adulterer as *"her man"* since he has made so many promises and was willing to be involved with her instead of his wife. When she becomes pregnant the sense of entitlement to call him hers may become more exaggerated. Maybe he promised her a visit and did not show or he promised to leave his wife that week but subsequently refused to go through with it. Many times the mistress' loyalty runs so deep that she may never go against him.

As far as *"motives"* go, an affair that leaves a child *"daddiless"* is one of the most awful circumstances imaginable, especially if the father already has children. Imagine how the mistress' child may feel when his or her father comes and goes because he is attempting to divide his time between two families. Some fathers may show up occasionally, trying to behave like dads. Others may make an effort to be involved and show an interest in their children's lives or education. These men may possibly make financial contributions, but never any significant attempts to influence their children's lives. For the most part, these mistress/mothers never really ask the fathers for much. In an unreasonable display of devotion, these women are not willing to *"interfere"* in the lives of the men they *"love"*. For some unknown reason, maybe because of her own pride or humiliation, she is not willing to expose or embarrass him to his other family. It is disturbing, but she is willing to keep his secret at any cost, even at the cost of her own child.

In many cases, these women never even ask for financial support for their children, nor do they hold these men accountable for any activities in the lives of these children. The father is permitted to miss birthdays, doctor's appointments, graduations and even sporting events. However, the mistress/mother tolerates all of these shortcomings in an effort to maintain his *"integrity"* with his family and to preserve his love for her.

Due to the mistress' undying dedication to *"her man"*, she will not violate his privacy despite the emotional impact it will have on their child. Ironically, this man is not subjected to any consequences from the mother and he is allowed to appear at his leisure. Maybe it's his flowery words or smooth talking that leaves her so caught up. It really does not make much sense, but these women are willing to let *"their men"* walk in and out of their lives. Regardless of his lack of involvement, he is allowed to return whenever he wants just to be welcomed with open arms. Maybe it's because of love or just stupidity, but nonetheless, this unexplainable behavior continues to happen.

The child, on the other hand, begins to resent the father as his repeated absences and broken promises become more familiar. The child's disrespect for their mother and father become the norm. As the child begins to act out and rebel against his or her mother and all that their father represents; he or she also starts to exhibit aggressive and sometimes abusive behavior toward the mother. The mothers become a target for negative behavior because she has been making excuses for the man the child has now come to despise. It becomes harder and harder for the child to respect this woman, his mother.

It's not difficult to understand why these children begin to lose respect for their mothers. In some cases, these women have taken part in perpetuating deception and have been willing participants in breaking up other women's homes. Even if she does not believe she is the actual cause for the breakup, she has still been a pawn in *"the game"*. For the most part, the mistress is perceived as a *"fool"* since she chose to be the *"other woman"* and play *"second string"* instead of being a starter. In the end, these children end up not having much of a relationship with their fathers but more than that, they tend to have contempt for their mothers. It is no wonder these children will likely rebel against both parents, which results in a *motive* for the child to possibly do wrong.

I feel this situation is one of the most heartbreaking because if the affair is discovered, it devastates two families not just one. The adulterer's wife and children are damaged right along with the mistress and her child. I mention the mistress and her child as a second thought because, in most cases, that's exactly what they are. Generally, the man's loyalties remain to his wife and their family together, so it is unlikely he will leave them for his *"jump off"*.

There is not enough that can be said about being the child of an adulterer. Historically, there was a scarlet letter placed upon the clothing of an adulteress to let everyone else know that she had been with another woman's husband. The scarlet letter that was traditionally associated with being the mistress of a married man has now been placed upon the woman's child as a result of an affair. The *"letter"* does not have to be physically present for it to exist. The absence of the child's father represents the letter that is stitched on the kid's heart. Every time the child has to explain why his or her father is not present at events; father-daughter dances; birthday parties; or school functions; the child really begins to feel the isolation and loneliness that goes along with being the bastard child of adulterers.

Regrettably, there are fathers who use the fact that their child was conceived during an affair as their *motive* for abandoning him or her. Many of these men rationalize deserting their children by blaming their mistresses for becoming pregnant. From his perspective he made his mistress aware of his intentions when they got together. He only wanted to have fun and there were not supposed to be any strings attached, especially not a baby. When she told him she was pregnant, his initial reaction was to ask if the child was his. The next response from him to her is generally for her to get rid of the child by having an abortion. He may even accuse her of attempting to trap him into having a long-term relationship with her by getting pregnant. He alleges she is deceiving him and this provides the *motive* he is looking for to walk out on her and the baby.

    The decision for these adulterous men to abandon their children and return to their families is simple for them. However, these guys never really consider the damage that is done to their illegitimate children. The pain that goes along with not having your biological father there for encouragement and support can be emotionally devastating. Additionally, the consequences for these fathers are greater than they might have considered when they decide to lie down with women who were not their wives. The truth of the matter is many men who have affairs are not thinking with the right parts of their anatomy. If these men would seriously contemplate all of the end results of their actions they might change their minds about having an affair. If a man thinks about the consequences of his actions he might realize the fact that he is not just cheating on his wife; he may end up cheating another child out of having a daddy. For some men the thought of making their mistresses pregnant is too remote to imagine. I just hope this chapter will plant a second thought in their minds so maybe some of the tragedies associated with being *daddiless* might be avoided.

Divorce as a "motive"

Differences of the heart and mind can lead two people, who may have loved one another at some point, down the path to divorce. Unfortunately, the end of a marriage can be another *"motive"* for some fathers to leave their children. Apparently, these men believe the divorce from their wives also equates to a divorce from their children.

Many times children become casualties of divorce wars between their parents. The bitterness that their mothers and fathers exhibit toward one another sometimes causes their children to believe that they are no longer loved. Divorce can bring out the worst in people. Anger, bitterness, and frustration are emotions that can be displayed during a divorce proceeding. With the lawyers fighting over trivial things like who will get the flat screen television or the silverware; the bickering back and forth can take a toll on both the husband

and wife pushing them toward the verge of hatred toward one another, that is, if they don't hate one another already.

In many divorces, one of the main points of contention is who will get custody of the children. The person who actually gets physical residential custody of the child is considered the *"custodial parent"*. Traditionally, custody was given to the child's mother because it was believed she would be more nurturing and caring toward the child. Today however, courts actually look at what living circumstances will be in the *"child's best interest."* That is not to say that women are granted custody any less. However, there are times when *"daddies"* are given custody nowadays and it is not just automatically given to the mother.

It is easy to understand why custody battles can be some of the worst parts of a divorce. Any parent that is worth anything is willing to fight for his or her children. This is not to say that those who are willing to compromise with their ex-spouses are considered worth less. It's just that most parents want their children with them and they want to raise the children themselves.

Fights for custody can get really dirty. All of the negative things that have taken place during the course of a marriage can be spilled out and are recorded for everyone in the courtroom to hear. Every lie that has been told; physical and emotional abuse; adultery; drug use; and alcoholism can become topics of discussion for the court to judge. It is the job of the court to determine what is in the *"best interest of the child"* after hearing the parents verbally tear one another apart. In many of these cases, the *"winner"* is the person who can paint the most unflattering picture of the other without going over the judge's imaginary tolerance line. So is there really a *"winner"* when a child has to choose between the two people they love and trust the most in the world? Even worse is the fact that the child generally does not get to make the decision as to who they want to be with. Sometimes, if the children are old enough, their feelings are taken into consideration, but ultimately the judge will make the decision.

After the divorce is finalized and the hearing is over, another power struggle begins. Having custody can result in a mother or father spitefully denying the other access to the child. In many cases, this denial is not legal. However, even with the court order in place, this does not mean access will be given immediately upon producing the divorce papers. In fact, it may require police involvement and many additional court appearances before the denied parent and child will be reunited. Sometimes the financial burden and aggravation can be too much for some people and they just give up. Is the frustration associated with fighting for his child, after a divorce, considered a sufficient reason for any father to give up on his child? There are actually some fathers who look for any excuse not to stick around. The divorce can provide the excuse they are looking for.

Maybe the *"blame game"* that goes on between some parents becomes his *"motive"* for leaving. Once the property is divided and the child support allotment is determined, next comes the *"blame game."* Obviously, the things that caused the divorce still resonate in the hearts and minds of both parents. The problem with either parent harboring ill will toward the other is that their biases and attitudes are observed by their children. In more cases than not, negative statements are made about the other parent out of anger and bitterness in order to extract revenge and to humiliate the former spouse. The negative comments are sometimes intended to damage the relationship between the child and the other parent. In other cases, the common hatred for this so called *"no good"* parent may possibly become the only bond that the *"good parent"* and the child may share.

At times the parent who has custody of the child can lead him or her to believe that their other parent could give less than a damn about them. This is not to say that some of the things these parents may say about their ex-spouses are not true. However, these kinds of statements can breed contempt for the child's other parent. It is true that contempt breeds contempt.

It is easy to see how one parent's negative opinions can be transferred to his or her children. Just think about it, after the trauma of watching their parents split up and decisions being made for them, it's understandable if these children take on the perspective of the parent they live with and oppose the one they do not reside with. There are always two sides to every story, but for a young, broken-hearted child, it is hard for him or her to understand why the non-custodial parent is not there.

The child may still believe his parent just gave up on them even if that parent put up the fight of their lives in an effort to get custody. Regrettably, there are custodial parents who are vindictive enough to allow their children to believe something that is not true. In fact, these parents are willing to add fuel to the flame by speaking negatively about the child's other parent and allowing the child to believe the other parent does not care about him or her. In the long run, if this *"bad parent"* cannot change the child's mind about him or her, this will result in a self-fulfilling prophecy. For some parents, there is only so much rejection, contempt, and disrespect they will tolerate from their children before they will just give up. Does it really make sense that some men will allow the negative *"motives"* of their ex-spouses to push them away from their children?

Even still, there are men who will allege that all the fighting that took place before, during, and after the divorce, led him to the conclusion that he needed a clean slate. But in the minds of these men, a clean slate may mean no wife and no kids. It's almost as if they believe the ties that bound them to their wives were also what connected them to their children. Nothing could be further from the truth for their children. The loyalties and affections a child has for its father is not so easily withdrawn, but given enough ammunition, it can be lost. It will take something drastic for these children to turn their backs on him.

Some men simply cannot deal with the pain associated with divorce. Maybe he was still in love with the child's mother and he could not stand to see his children raised by some other man. Conversely, there are men who will start a new family and forget about his other children before the ink can dry on the divorce papers. He begins to disregard his original family or he attempts to blend the old and the new. Siblings already have enough trouble sharing their parents with their natural brothers and sisters; it's understandable how difficult and awkward it must be for the children to share their father with another woman's kids. I'm sure these children feel like someone stole their daddy.

For children it can be difficult to come to terms with the fact that their father now has a new family. Adding to this frustration is the knowledge that they will now have to share their father with someone else. All of the attention they were accustom to getting from *"their daddy"* is now gone. There are children who will question themselves and wonder what was so wrong with them or their family? Why would their father slight them and find another family more likable than theirs? The most significant question is why must the children suffer as a consequence of their parents' inability to make their relationships work?

The commitment that existed between the husband and wife was expected to translate into a similar commitment to their children. It was anticipated that these relationships would be forever, not just for as long as it was convenient. Overall, if a man does decide to leave his wife it would seem somewhat easier for him to leave her as opposed to his children. Think about it, there is only a contract between the husband and wife. On the other hand, the child is his flesh and blood, made partly from his DNA, and he is still willing to just walk away. If there were any connection between him and the child it would appear that giving up on his blood relative would be extremely difficult.

Is it possible for a father to *"fall out of love"* with his child in the same way some men and women claim to *"fall out of love"* with their spouses? The way that some children are treated after a divorce gives the impression that the love their fathers once had for them is gone when the divorce occurs. Is this just a defense mechanism? Is this just his way of coping with the fact that his family will be broken up? It is really a shame that the irreconcilable differences that these parents have with one another will become the source of their child's pain. Divorce is war for some people and the children become *"collateral damage",* the unintended victims of the battle. These kids suffer from the long-lasting wounds and scars caused by this fight. There are children who never recover from their parents' separation and go through life attempting to fill the voids they've experienced. They are the casualties of war and unfortunately, some men consider them acceptable losses.

There are many reasons people get divorced: adultery, abuse, money, or they just fell out of love. Whatever the reason, if it leaves a child *daddiless* it may possibly push the child in a negative way *(motive)* or a positive way *(motivation)*. How will the child react to this situation is really a paramount question? Will he believe his parents will get back together and daddy will return? Will she rebel against the parent that is or is not present? Will the child blame herself for the divorce? Will his grades drop, or will she become an overachiever, hoping this will be the action that reunites her family? What will happen if and when the children's efforts are not successful? Will they go out looking for a family connection or love in the streets by joining a gang? Will promiscuity become their way of adapting? Will they go out and shoot up their school? Will they commit suicide or give it serious thought? Will they become better children to the parent that they have with them every day or will they cause them problems? All of these things are potential outcomes from the loss of a parent through divorce.

By no means am I suggesting that a couple should stay together for the sake of the children. However, I hope parents consider the impact that their separation will have on their kids before, during, and after the divorce. If it's possible to maintain a positive relationship or reduce the negative impact on the child, I would hope that both parents would consider those options as opposed to just walking away. The resentment and anger that is felt may make it extremely hard for parents to forgive one another, but that should not be a reason to leave their child.

Losing access to a parent may be either a *motive* or a *motivation* for a child because there is anger, self-hatred, blame, frustration, and grief that go along with this deprivation. It is important for fathers to realize that their absences have the potential to be extremely destructive *motives* for their children. For offspring subjected to these situations, it is important that they realize despite the absence of a father they can still control their destinies and use the divorce as a *motivation* to do well. Once they get past the heartbreak of their parents' split, hopefully, they will learn to recognize that they still have the ability to release themselves of the burdens they did not create. Parents supporting and communicating with their children can help them to cope with the changes that occur as a result of a divorce. More importantly, parents need to realize they can play a very important role in whether or not the divorce will be a *motive vs.* a *motivation b*ecause children will generally follow the examples of their parents. Thus, if parents exemplify hatred and disrespect toward one another, their children may possibly copy this behavior. So be positive and lead by example. When possible and appropriate, speak positively about your former spouse and let the child know that forgiveness will help to ease the pain they may be feeling.

Chapter VII.

WHAT WAS HIS MOTIVE FOR LEAVING?

Why did he leave? If you noticed in the title of this chapter, I characterized the father leaving as a *motive* issue. Meaning it had to be something negative that prompted him to leave. I characterized it in this way because there is not a situation in my mind where it is justifiable for a father to leave his child. Whether it is a divorce; a one-night stand; a disagreement with the mother; child support; prison; or abuse; it's all negative.

At this point, I think it is important to mention that even though I am advocating for fathers to be involved in their children's lives, if a father is abusive toward his child or the child's mother, it is best for her to take the kids as far away from him as possible. I have to acknowledge that certain situations are just so toxic that they may not produce any positive results. I am not saying that these situations are hopeless, however, unless and until he gets some help for whatever is causing him to abuse his family he should not be allowed in their lives. Despite my feelings, there is still the negative taint that goes along with the absence of these fathers. Even though the child's safety and well-being are intact, the situation is still undesirable overall because this just leaves another child *daddiless*. So even in abuse situations where the father is taken out of the child's life for an absolutely valid reason, the negative *motive of* the father can still impact on his *daddiless* child.

So why did he leave? This question has haunted the minds and souls of millions of people whose fathers have left or were never a part of their children's lives. As a defense mechanism, some men and woman may display a cavalier attitude when they convey that their father's absence does not matter to them. Some may suggest that they have moved on with their lives and are over prior disappointments. *"He doesn't owe me anything"* is a common expression for those who have *"overcome"* their *daddiless* problem.

Personally, I wanted to know the reason why he was not there. In many ways, I desired an explanation for why I had to grow up without my father. For many of us an explanation is the least that he can do. Some children go so far as to blame themselves for his absence. The one thing I knew for sure was that it was not something that I did that made him leave. It is so important that these children know definitively that it was not anything they might have done to cause this. In many instances, it was his decision and his selfishness that precipitated the abandonment of his child. It is also crucial to understand that there is no one answer that will fit every situation. One father's reason for not remaining with his kids may be completely different from another.

It's apparent that some fathers have no problem with not knowing their children. For me, I cannot imagine any day of my life when I would want to wake up and not know where my children are or wonder if they are safe. Therefore, the idea of leaving my children voluntarily seems unfathomable. As a man, I have heard many stories from fathers who have never had relationships with their children. The reasons for this lack of interaction run the gamut. What is extremely unfortunate, but nonetheless true, is the fact that it is no longer an isolated incident for a father to leave his child or children. On the contrary, the absence of a father in a household has become the norm and is extremely prevalent, more prevalent than even having a father who is present. The *daddiless* issue has risen to the point that it has become the punchline for many jokes. For example, the statement *"You aren't my daddy!"* is usually followed up with the question, *"Are you?"* This comedic dialogue makes light of the fact that there are a considerable number of children today who don't have a clue who their fathers might be. Nonetheless, society still downplays this epidemic. People in American society have gone so far as to simply change the makeup of what constitutes a family. Instead of continuing to look for men to play their part as fathers others have been inserted into their roles. Traditional notions of what a family should look like have gone by the wayside.

Moreover, the issue of a father leaving his child transcends all racial, economic, class, and social lines. The *daddiless* child may be black, white, Hispanic, Asian, boy, girl, rich, poor, from a trailer park or the suburbs. This phenomenon can happen to anyone living anywhere. Many factors can contribute to a man's unwillingness or inability to stay around. For some men any excuse will do, but for other fathers this section provides an accurate portrayal of their reason for being absent. I hope that this book will let them know that their situations are not unique and their *motives* for leaving still are not justified. I just wonder how many of these individuals contemplated the effect that leaving would have on their offspring.

Whether you were fighting for custody during a divorce proceeding and lost, or the baby's mother used to beat your behind, one should never quit the fight for your child. One caveat to this is if your presence in the child's life will be more negative or destructive than positive and productive. If that's the case then you should stay away because the child is better off without you. For example, if you believe that physical violence or emotional abuse is acceptable then it is best that you stay away.

Hopefully, these individuals are willing to acknowledge their destructive behavior and just stay away. I would suggest that these men send a letter instead of trying to meet their children in person. At least this will let the child know that their father thought enough of them to provide an explanation of why he left without making the rest of the family uncomfortable. If you are the father in a situation where you have been abusive and the family wants nothing to do with you or you have no way of knowing where your child is, I recommend that you write the letter anyway. Maybe one day you will have an opportunity to send it to the child, but more than that, it may help you acknowledge your faults and start your personal rehabilitation.

Let's explore a few of the *motives* fathers present as justification for leaving their children. Some fathers claim to have been *"trapped"* by their baby's mothers and they insist it was necessary to disappear. These men claim they left because they did not want to be forced into fatherhood. When you hear these stories it sounds like a hostage situation or something. It's like a dramatic fictional story where a man's sperm was kidnapped and forcibly injected into a woman and she ended up pregnant. Maybe it was the old turkey baster scam.

I know there are women out there who see a good thing and are willing to do anything to get what they want. Whether it's a guy's money, his good looks, or the woman's desire to be a mother, she will do whatever it takes to achieve her objective. Nevertheless, in some cases this *motive* is hard to believe because the man is denying his responsibility in the sexual relationship. The story goes something like this. "*Man, I just met this chick and she gave up the booty on the first date, the condom broke and she told me that she didn't want to have an abortion. I wasn't going to get caught up with some chick that I didn't even know and raise this kid. Hell, I didn't even know if the kid was mine or not. If she gave it to me on the first date who is to say she did not give it to some other guy.*" How about this one, "We *had been dating for a while and she told me she was on birth control, but in reality she had stopped taking her pills. I wasn't ready for a kid and she knew it, but that was her way of keeping me. So when I found out about it I jetted.*" Are these just cop outs *(motives)* or are they real and true situations?

Needless to say, in some cases the issues with these mothers are real and not just cop-outs. Personally, I know of two specific situations where the issues were legitimate and the reasons these men left were somewhat understandable. We cannot be ignorant to the fact that there are women who will scheme and plot to keep men or at least get on the proverbial *"gravy train."* Men need to keep in mind that in every situation, regardless of who the woman may be or what she may have said, you must be ready to step up and handle your responsibilities. That's a harsh reality that some men don't want to acknowledge. As men, we have to be ready to take accountability for our actions instead of leaving the situation for women to handle alone.

Sometimes a bombshell can be dropped in a man's lap and they don't know what hit them. For example, I know of a situation where a couple had been married for almost 12 years when unexpectedly a woman that the husband dated years earlier contacted him alleging he was the father of her child. The man had no idea that the woman he was involved with so many years ago was even pregnant; let alone by him. He later confirmed that the teenage child was in fact his daughter.

In another case, there was a man who had been happily married for about two years and one day he received a letter from the Child Support Enforcement Agency. The letter ordered the man to court and informed him that he would be subjected to a DNA test. The woman he dated prior to his marriage believed that he was the father of her child. This situation was compounded by the fact that the woman incorrectly identified a number of men as being the child's father before she arrived at this man. The man took the test then learned he had a two-year-old daughter. The culmination of the scenario was that this new revelation played a part in ruining his marriage, as well as, set the stage for a strange and unfamiliar relationship with his daughter. So now, he's paying child support and the mother wants to act as if he was the person who wronged her. She uses the child as a pawn attempting to deny him access to visitation even though there is a court order that says he is entitled to spend time with his little girl.

In both situations, the men who found out about their children subsequently accepted their responsibilities by attempting to become intricate parts of their children's lives. One problem in these situations is that the children may question why their mothers did not inform their fathers about the pregnancies. In some cases, the son or daughter will blame the mother, but in others, he or she may have the perception that their father was not worth informing. What kind of an image is that for a child to have of his or her father? If the father is vilified throughout their child's life, he or she may become so embittered and angry based upon their mother's depiction of him that the child may not ever want anything to do with his father. It is not uncommon for these men to assert that it was entirely the mother's fault that he left. Either she was too possessive, jealous or they were simply incompatible and never in love, all these arguments tend to be made as justification for his actions.

Other fathers claim that "B*aby daddy drama*" is the culprit that led him to leave. There are unfortunate situations where a woman is involved with a man who is jealous of her child's father. In these situations, the father is ready, willing and able to be present for his child to contribute in every way possible. However, the mother's companion does not like the daddy coming around. The boyfriend thinks that the father and the child's mother still have a romantic connection. In many of these situations, nothing could be further from the truth. The father only wants to be with his child and the mother desires to facilitate that interaction. Nonetheless, this overly protective, insecure, over possessive boyfriend tries to sabotage visitation because "*his girl*" and the child's father are thought to be sneaking around behind his back. Sometimes extreme measures have to be taken to prevent a fight between the father of the child and the current man in the mother's life. It sounds ridiculous but it still happens.

Chapter VIII.

BABY MAMA DRAMA

"*Baby mama drama*" is similar to the over possessive boyfriend scenario. The *"daddy"* wants to be in his child's life, but the baby's mama either still wants him or is jealous of the fact that he has moved on with another woman. The mother throws up roadblocks that prevent the *"daddy"* from being a part of his child's life. For example, when the *"daddy"* attempts to pick up his child for a visit, the mother may refuse to provide the child with clean clothes or no clothes at all. She will simply tell the daddy that the child needs new clothes and this is his opportunity to contribute. This ploy is a means of extracting money even if he is paying child support. The action may be a power trip for some mothers because the child support is more than enough for her to purchase new clothes for the child.

In other situations the mother may want the father to *"play daddy"* to children who are not his own. For example, if a mother has multiple children and different *"baby daddies"*, she may expect the one father who is paying child support to carry the financial weight for her other children. Sadly, it's as if the mother thinks she hit the jackpot with the one man who is willing to fulfill his responsibilities. I recall a situation where a *"dad"* went to pick up his daughter for a visit. The child's mother told the dad that he needed to take all of her children with him or he would not be able to take his own daughter for a visit. None of the other children were his but he was made to feel that he was responsible for them because she did not want the other kids to feel slighted. Whenever he would go over to spend time with his child he was told to play with the other kids. He was not intentionally trying to disregard these other children, but she was forcing him to *"play daddy"*. All he wanted to do was spend time with his daughter. How fair is that? Needless to say, the situation got old very fast.

Let's take the circumstances a step further, consider a father goes to pick up his child with his new wife or girlfriend and the child's mother gets jealous, refusing to allow him to take the child with him. The baby's mama's tactic might be to pick a fight with the new wife or girlfriend by exaggerating a situation that may have occurred with the child. She places the dad in an awkward situation of trying to maintain the peace between all parties involved. Understandably, a mother does not want her child to be subjected to a lot of different women when a father may be dating, but again eliminating access altogether is not reasonable. More importantly a woman should not try and control the man or his love life by using the child to dictate his relationships.

What happens if the mother of the man's child still wants him in her life? Sometimes she will resort to slashing car tires or busting out windows as a means of expressing her frustration. These actions could result in police involvement, constant court filings for civil protection orders, requests for increases in child support or complications during visits. All of this insanity can be enough to keep a lesser man away, but a true *"daddy"* is always willing to keep fighting for his children, no matter what.

Chapter IX.

THE TRAP

Under the law, there is a legal defense of *"entrapment"* in criminal cases. Black's Law Dictionary defines *"entrapment"* as *"the act of officers or agents of the government in inducing a person to commit a crime not contemplated by him, for the purpose of instituting a criminal prosecution against him."* The Black's Law Dictionary also defines the word *"entrap"* as *"to catch, to entrap, to ensnare; hence to catch by artifice. To involve in difficulties or distresses; to catch or involve in contradictions."*

What's ironic about the defense of *"entrapment"* is that *"daddiless"* children use it when they get into trouble with the law. At the same time, some of the fathers who decide to leave their children use the same defense as their reason for walking out on their kids. Even though there are no *"officers or government agents"* involved, at least not until child support is sought, some of them still feel a crime has been committed against them. Many of these men would say they have been *"caught, entrapped, ensnared; and involved in difficulties and distresses"* at the hands of deceptive women. They would argue that these women have subjected them to *"contradictions."* In many cases, the unwanted child is considered the *"contradiction."* One person may want the child while the other person doesn't want anything to do with their offspring. Nobody wants to be caught in a so-called *"trick bag"* and a child should never be used as a pawn in a plot of lies and deception.

We all know there are scheming and conniving people in this world. These opportunistic individuals are willing to do whatever it takes to get who or what they want. Unfortunately, this is true for men and woman who want to control or manipulate others for whatever reason. Throughout history, pregnancy has been used as a tool to achieve these negative objectives.

Honestly, the issue of pregnancy should be on both a man and woman's mind when they engage in sexual intercourse. The thing is, for some men and women this is all too true, actually, pregnancy is all that is on their minds. The objective for these individuals is to become pregnant or to impregnate someone. The *motives* for these people vary from person to person. Some of them are just selfish and want what they want when they want it. Others crave money or desire some form of financial gain. Alternatively, there are women who simply yearn to have a child and they don't care who they trap to achieve their goal. Pregnancy has even been used as a form of leverage or revenge to get back at ex-lovers. These are extreme situations and trapping someone into becoming a parent is never positive.

Imagine for a moment being the person that has been tricked and trapped in any of these situations. Ask yourself, what generally happens to any animal or a person who has been ensnared or feels like it's trapped or boxed in a corner? It can be expected that even the most timid animal or person will attack when ensnared. In many situations, they can be quite ferocious and the attack will generally be made against the trapper, but it can also be taken out on innocent bystanders as well. In the case of a man or woman who feels trapped by an unwanted pregnancy, the attack can even be against the unwanted child. This may result in violence or resentment toward the child that can ultimately have negative consequences for both the parent and the unwanted offspring.

The feelings of being trapped are compounded by feelings of being tricked. A great deal of anger and frustration will be experienced by the person who has been deceived into having a child they did not want. This can result in abuse directed toward the unwelcomed child. With anger, frustration, resentment and possibly abuse being exhibited by the mother, the father, or both against the child, the overall consequence will be that the trap may become a *motive* for one or both of the parents to abandon the child. Alternatively, if they do stay, the negative treatment the child receives will have lasting effects. Most likely, the child's behavior will manifest itself in a variety of adverse ways either toward others or through self-destructive activities. This negative treatment by their parents may very well become a *motive* for the child in the future. Therefore, the consequences of this undesired pregnancy may become a *motive* for both the parents and the child. In many ways, resentment will beget resentment.

Chapter X.

TOO YOUNG, TOO SCARED, TOO MUCH RESPONSIBILITY

It takes a great deal of maturity and courage to be a daddy, not so much to be a father. I recall the day my wife came home with a greeting card that said *"Congratulations you're a Dad"*. I was in my second year of law school and did not have a clue about what we needed to do or how we were going to manage financially. At the same time, I was excited about the prospect of being a parent. More than anything, I knew I wanted to be more involved than my father had been.

I was 27 years old when I received the news I was going to be a daddy. One of the first thoughts that went through my mind was, "I'm too young to be a father." How could I be responsible for someone else's life when I was still navigating being responsible for my own? Nonetheless, I was going to be a dad and I had to *"man up"* to the challenge.

Unlike some men, I was married when I learned we were having a child. Knowing I had someone in my life who was willing to share in the responsibility of caring for our child made the situation appear much more manageable. There is a degree of comfort that can be drawn from knowing you will not be alone raising a child. Being married can help in providing some relief especially when you are having a baby with someone you love and who loves you. It can be reassuring to know that there is another person who will hold themselves accountable for the work associated with raising your child. Sometimes being in a committed relationship can reduce some of the anxiety and fear related to becoming a new parent. Many men want to have children with their wives and this may help to create a positive environment for both the mother and the father.

That does not mean that the timing of the pregnancy is not important. I came to realize that there is no ideal age or perfect time to have a child. Young or old; rich or poor; the point that really matters is the level of maturity that a person has reached when considering the decision to have a child. Many people believe the philosophy, *"with age comes maturity"*; however, I'm certain we all know individuals that are well beyond the age of adulthood who still act immature. The reality is a person's age is no excuse to claim that staying and raising a child is not feasible.

I have known many young girls who have accepted their responsibilities as mothers despite the fact that they were still in high school or even middle school. It has been said girls mature faster than boys do and these situations tend to confirm this point. Many of these girls may not have been the best mothers but at least they stepped up and made the effort.

Obviously, these young women were scared by the prospect of having a child, however many young woman have been able to overcome their fears to take on the responsibility of being a mother. Being afraid is a natural reaction for any parent and it does not diminish with age. The parental concerns do not subside completely; they just evolve as the parent and the child grow older.

I believe the thought of making decisions affecting the life of another human being can be intimidating for a person of any age. Fear can be paralyzing or it can result in running away; therefore, certain men will not do anything and simply ignore the birth or life of their child, while others opt to run away. There is no shame if a father is a bit apprehensive about parenthood. If you embrace the fact that we are not perfect and we will make mistakes, you will obtain a degree of peace as you embark on your journey as a parent.

GOD in his infinite wisdom knew that we would need some time to adjust to the idea of having a baby. He allows the mother and father nine months to prepare for the arrival of their child. I believe GOD gave us this time in order to reduce some of the anxiety that comes along with finding out we are going to be parents. For some, this time will ignite the fight or flight reflexes that we all have. Isn't your child worth fighting for?

Being a parent has been one of the most challenging endeavors in my life. Although I was afraid, I did not allow my fear to prevent me from trying. Yes, I have made some mistakes, but I would not have learned from my missteps had I not embraced the opportunity. My experiences as a father have brought me wisdom and courage. So do not let the *motive* of being too young or too scared become the reason that you walk away from your child. Just think, this child is entering into this world dependent on his father and mother to survive and without them, he or she may not make it. As a new mom or dad, you will not realize your strengths or weaknesses as a parent until you make the effort. Please understand I am not advocating for people to have children if they are not ready. On the contrary, I would recommend waiting until you are in a secure and loving relationship, preferably married, before having a child. However, if you find yourself in a situation where you are going to be a new parent, don't run away because you're afraid, don't run away because you think you're too young or too irresponsible. Don't run away at all. Just know you will become more mature and some of your fears will subside as you go through the parenting experience.

One of the main points to be made here is that fear of the unknown can wreak havoc on a person's mind. This is one of the major reasons that men will jump ship as opposed to raising their children. In order to address these fears it is important to learn as much as possible about being a parent. Don't allow pride or inexperience to lead you away from possibly one of the greatest opportunities in life. Explore the possibilities and do not let fear be the determining factor for you.

Chapter XI.

A WOMAN CAN'T TEACH A BOY HOW TO BE A MAN

Most people today have heard the old African proverb *"it takes a village to raise a child."* This proverb became popular in mainstream America by Hillary Clinton, the wife of former President Bill Clinton. This proverb says everything that needs to be said about what is necessary to give a child a chance to live a positive life. For the most part, a child needs more than what a single mother may have to give in order to raise a child properly. Raising a child consists of uplifting him or her, not just rearing, bringing up, or nurturing them; it requires more than what one person has to offer. Raising a child requires the input of both men and women in order to create the necessary balance for a child to be well-rounded. Maybe the man does not have to be the child's father, but it does require a man's input.

Today, there are an overwhelming number of women raising children on their own. Recently, I was watching a news report that was somewhat surprising, but not so much in this day and age. The reporter came on and said, a survey had been completed and about forty percent of Americans felt that marriage was becoming obsolete. *"Obsolete!"* "Meaning *outdated or no longer necessary."* Therefore, what this study appears to be saying is the sanctity of marriage is now something that is trivial or pointless in our society. For many of us this is disturbing. It gives the impression that the traditional concept of family has just been thrown out of the window. The idea of a nuclear family made up of a man, a woman, and their children has fallen by the wayside. Even more prevalent today is the belief that a man is no longer needed to raise a well-balanced child. While the term well-balanced may be relative, it is important for parents to understand that both men and women contribute to the overall development of each child. There are masculine and feminine traits that are passed on to every child by their parents. These characteristics have to be cultivated and developed. However, if one parent exhibits too much control or influence the child may become confused about the roles of each parent. Realistically, no one parent has all of the answers to every question presented by a child.

To be honest, (no offense to the single mothers reading this book) but a woman cannot teach a boy how to be a man. I am sure there are many single mothers that will disagree with what I am saying and that is okay. Nevertheless, a boy will never know how to relate to other men if he does not have a male influence in his life. The fact of the matter is there are some things that are inherent to men that can only be taught to a boy by a man. For example, a woman cannot teach a boy how to be a father. A woman cannot teach a boy what it is like to be a man. She cannot explain the reason why "m*en are from one planet and women from another*", maybe no one can. No matter how hard a woman may try, she simply cannot be a man.

Growing up in a single parent household, I had an opportunity to see how difficult it can be for a mother trying to raise her children on her own. My favorite West Coast gangsta rapper said it best in his 1995 song about "M*amas*". He explained that when things would go wrong he and his sister would blame their mother. Think about this for a moment, if there is no other parent in your household who else would get the blame but "*mama?*" This was true in my household. When the gas was turned off in the middle of the winter, or when the welfare check did not come, it was all *"mama's"* fault. We would blame her for almost everything. When she had a boyfriend that we did not like or when we could not afford the newest clothes, she would hear about it.

My mother did the best she could and she did a good job at raising three boys on her own. It was not without some trials and tribulations, but without her courage and street smarts, I would not be the man I am today. Even with all of her strength and determination, my mother could not instruct me on what was necessary to be a man. Some of the challenges and circumstances we faced with our mother helped to transform us from boys to men, but we still needed male role models to help guide our way.

Without a father, being there to give us advice or to help financially, my eldest brother stepped up and showed my brother and I the direction we should go in as men. He did not specifically say, *"I am teaching you these things and this will help to make you a man."* He did something better, he led by example. He got a job at an early age and by doing this, he imparted upon us a strong work ethic. He helped buy food when we were hungry, pay the bills when they needed to be paid, and he even taught us a few things about dating girls, even though my middle brother was considered the *"ladies man."* However, one of the most important things my eldest brother did for us was demonstrate what it meant to be responsible and not to rely on anyone else to give us what we needed. If he wanted something, he would go to work and get it. My brother's independence taught us what it meant to be self-sufficient and self-confident, which are both qualities that are necessary for a boy to become a man. These are also the characteristics necessary to turn a *"motive"* into a *"motivation."*

Just because a boy's father is not in his life does not mean he cannot develop as a man. Regardless of whether he acts like it or not, from a legal perspective, the world is going to view this boy as a man when he turns 18 years old. In reality, he will not truly become a man until he *"handles his business"* as a man. Some misguided boys and young men come to believe that making a baby makes them men. Conceiving a child does not make a boy a man; a baby does not even have to be a part of the equation for a man to behave as a man. However, if a boy does impregnate a girl, he will not be considered a man until he takes responsibility for himself and the child. Once he gets involved in this way he will truly be viewed as a man. A boy cannot live at home with his mama and think he is now a man just because he helped to create a baby. It takes more than dropping a seed in the forest to plant a tree; it must be cultivated in fertile soil in order for it to grow. The same principle applies to a boy making a baby; his responsibility is just starting at conception.

Children blame others for the things they do and for the things that happen to them. One thing that distinguishes a boy from a man is being accountable. A true man will *"step up"* and acknowledge what he has done when he makes a mistake, while a boy will point a finger and say it was someone else's fault. At times even blaming all of his problems on the absence of his father. This explanation may be acceptable early in life but as a child gets older it just does not work. I'll talk more about what it means to be a man a little later.

HYPERSENSITIVITY

Some of the characteristics I saw in my mother when I was a boy have affected me as a man. I do not know if these responses or feelings were *"taught"* to me by my mother. Can one person teach another person how to feel? Maybe not, but I know that in some ways a person can teach others how they should react in a given situation. A child will emulate the things that they see, even various emotions. I believe I emulated some of my mother's actions and reactions; I internalized them and made them my own.

One of the things that I found out about myself is that I am hypersensitive (or what some would consider overly sensitive). I do not know if this exists in other children who have grown up with their mothers (as the sole parent), but this is my reality. I believe this is a characteristic I *"learned"* from my mother. She is an emotional person and her feelings can be hurt very easily. Don't get me wrong, she is a very tough woman, but she is also very caring and her concern for others sometimes causes her pain. Some of the battles and abuse that I saw her go through may have elevated and changed the way I respond to others. For example, I have a tendency to feel as though others are disrespecting me in some of the most trivial matters. I do not fly off the handle at every little thing, but I do find myself exhibiting anger and not managing it well. For many years, I found myself yelling and screaming in an effort to find *"my voice"*. I did not know how to express myself without getting loud and angry. During that time, I never felt like anyone was listening to me or that my opinion counted. Maybe part of it was because I was the youngest child, but I also believe that some of my anger management issues stem from me being *daddiless*. In many ways, I believe this is part of my own personal *"motive."*

My mother did her best to correct me when I acted out or engaged in inappropriate behavior. At times, she put the fear of GOD in me. When I was a child the old saying, *"I brought you into this world and I will take you out"* was used frequently in our household. My middle brother was usually the catalyst for us hearing that statement. My mother worked very hard to correct our behavior, but after we reached a certain age, it took my eldest brother to knock the *"you know what"* out of us a couple of times before we got back in line.

Not to sound stereotypical, but the discipline and correction of a man, especially a father, can be a game changer. There will come a time when a boy will begin to believe he is stronger than his father and wiser than his parents. My mother would say this was the time when boys start to *"smell"* themselves; this time was usually around puberty. These boys will begin to challenge their parents' authority and test the boundaries to see what they can and cannot get away with. When this happens, matters can culminate and result in very explosive situations. If the wrong person is involved in addressing these situations it can result in disaster.

Discipline is an extremely important part of any child's life. A lack of discipline can cause a child to be unruly. On the other hand, too much discipline can lead to rebellion. There has to be a balance, a good mix of discipline and nurturing. If one element is emphasized more than the other, this can result in an imbalance in the child's development. In a *"healthy"* situation, both the mother and the father can create the necessary equilibrium of punishment and reward. Each parent will also have an opportunity to participate in both the praises and penalties for their children. Most of the time mothers are expected to provide the nurturing, while fathers provide the discipline. When one parent is absent (from the child's life), the other will have to take on both roles.

My mother was both the disciplinarian and the praise giver. There was no one else there to play *"good cop"* when she had to play *"bad cop"*. Moreover, if there had been a man around, we might have tested her a lot less than we did. When I got upset, I would lash out at my mother. I was not an unruly child. Most of the time I was a good kid, but I was an extremely *"mouthy"* person. I liked to consider myself *"outspoken,"* not *"mouthy."* I was constantly questioning my mother and *"back talking"*. Since my oldest brother was five years older than I was, he was away at college for most of my teenage years. During those years, I gave my mother a great deal of problems exercising my *"outspokenness"*. My children have not reached their teenage years yet, but I am sure that there is no greater frustration for a parent than a *"back talking"* teenager. I know that if there would have been a man in the house, my behavior would have been toned down about ten times. I experienced this when my eldest brother came home from college (on break), he saw how I was talking back to my mother and put his *"foot in my behind"*.

    I did not realize it then, but I know now that I was doing whatever I felt like I could get away with. As I have grown, I have concluded that some of my anger issues stem from my father's absence. This conclusion sounds somewhat cliché considering many people blame the negative aspect of their lives on the absence of their fathers. I was angry for no apparent reason or at least that was what I thought at the time. I realized later that my anger was partly because my father was gone and without fatherly boundaries I lacked discipline. He was not there to help address my inappropriate behavior or stop me from questioning my mother's authority. I would act out from a place of anger more often than not because I did not have him there to punish me or chastise me to get me back in line. Mom did not let me get away with everything, but I was her *"baby boy"* and as a result, she would let some behaviors slide. As a guy, I am sure a man would have addressed my behavior much more firmly. There seems to be a difference between how a mother and a father discipline a child.

It is strange how a person can miss something they have never known. When I would see my friends or relatives enjoying their fathers or when I watched a family on television, there was a longing for that kind of relationship. Maybe the envy that I felt for that type of connection is where some of my anger originated. I'm sure there are many children who feel that same kind of jealousy and anger, whether they know their fathers or not.

In addition to my anger and envy issues, there were other sources of my hypersensitivity. It was hard for me to get over the feelings of abandonment and rejection that I felt. There was no way for my mother to fulfill my desire for acceptance or my desire to be liked by others. Fortunately, those negative feelings were *motivation* for me and I converted them into positive energy to prove any naysayer wrong about kids like me. Just because we were left by our fathers does not mean we were left behind altogether.

I have experienced some degree of insecurity in relationships with others, but that did not prevent me from continuing to strive to achieve more than anyone ever thought I could. More than anything, I really believe that growing up as a young man, who was raised by a woman, has affected how I address situations. Being raised solely by a woman allowed me to be *"more in touch with my feminine side."* I know how to be sensitive and caring, along with being compassionate and kind. While I learned to be charming and desirable, I had to put forth more effort towards things that were traditionally masculine, like lifting weights or playing sports; these were things my mother could not teach me. Learning how to talk to the opposite sex and not being shy about it was a challenge. In spite of never feeling comfortable about engaging females, I did find my beautiful wife.

Despite my insecurities and inexperience, there were certain topics like puberty and sex that were open for discussion with my mother. When we engaged in those conversations, it felt rather awkward mainly because my brothers and I were talking about females with our mother.

For many of us, if not most men, learn how to be men from men. Fortunately, I was blessed to have two older brothers whom I observed and learned from. Some children do not have older male siblings like I did. My brother's life experiences taught me a great deal about the do's and don'ts of life. So many young men get confused about their identity if they do not have that male figure to guide them along the way. They may make mistakes when addressing women, committing crimes against them, or become overly aggressive in their interaction mainly because they are not aware of appropriate boundaries. To clarify, just because a father is absent does not at all mean a child will become a deviant person. However, the guidance of a father, along with witnessing positive relationships between men and women, will help to establish appropriate limits.

Another aspect about being hypersensitive is that emotions can be easily elevated, which can be both positive and negative. Being more aware of and sensitive to other people's feelings is a positive aspect of hypersensitivity. On the other hand, adverse results can occur because one is overly sensitive. It can lead someone to be presumptuous about how someone else may feel in a situation. The presumptions about another person's feeling can be completely wrong and this can lead to misunderstandings. Imputing feelings upon another person that they are not experiencing can really cause frustration in relationships. I know this to be true because I find myself telling my wife, *"you shouldn't be upset about that"*, or *"you're angry aren't you?"* Even if that may not have been how she actually felt, I would insist that she did. That may have been the way I would have felt if the situation happened to me, but who am I to tell her how she should feel? No one wants to be told what emotions they are experiencing, especially if the description is inaccurate.

A hypersensitive person can be prone to allow others to provoke improper responses from them. There has always been a stigma associated with men being overly emotional. The myth is that women are meant to demonstrate their emotions while men are expected to keep their emotions buried. It is not considered macho or strong to be emotional as a man. *"Real men don't cry"* is an old adage that many men still follow. I am not certain why some of society think that men showing emotions makes them weak or somehow less of a man. Men who express their emotions may tend to live longer more fulfilling lives and probably cope with stress better because they release the tension, anger, sadness, and other emotions they experience. There is tremendous strength in being brave enough to express your true sentiments. I know mothers can teach boys how to be expressive; my mother did. To be honest, if she had prevented me from speaking my mind, I may not have become an attorney.

From my perspective, my back talking and rebelliousness lead me down a positive path. Let me make a point here of saying that I am not encouraging children to be disrespectful toward their parents; however it is not always inappropriate to ask questions when you don't understand something. There was a silver lining in my defiance in that my negative *motive* (anger), became a positive *motivation* (advocacy for others). Again, I was able to use my father's absence and the things that went along with it to my advantage.

I believe the tendency to be overly sensitive is more prevalent in the *daddiless* population. That may be the reason that some of us try harder to make our relationships work, even when they are toxic. At times, we may overreact when outcomes are not in our favor; some individuals can be explosive or even overbearing because of their extreme passion. However, if they have the right person in their lives they can be extremely loving and that passion can be expressed in the right ways as well.

Alternatively, this high sensitivity level has frequently been utilized in court cases when a person conveys he grew up without his father. This particular *motive* is a lot more prevalent in crimes of passion. It is argued that a certain behavior or response provoked the individual to react the way they did. Hypersensitivity can be a significant contributor to domestic violence in some relationships. Feelings of jealousy, disrespect, or a lack of trust are sometimes enhanced by overly sensitive individuals. Escalated responses to circumstances can even lead to murder or suicide in some cases. I know this phenomenon is real because I have dealt with some of these negative emotions and so have many of you who are reading this book.

If a person does not know how to control their level of agitation, it can control them. This then becomes another *motive or motivation situation*. While I still experience moments of being overly sensitive about some issues, I am improving by recognizing my feelings and addressing the source of the matter promptly. I am not presenting hypersensitivity as a justification for certain behaviors, but as a relevant factor.

Later, I will explain some of the events that contributed to my hypersensitivity as well as how those occurrences helped to *motivate* me as opposed to allowing it to continue to be one of my *motives*.

Overall, women teaching boys how to be men without a male influence is virtually impossible. There has to be a male example of some kind to create the right balance for the child. Growing up I learned many wonderful things from my mother, some characteristics would be considered more feminine than others, for example being extra sensitive. The point is, raising a well-rounded child requires both male and female influences.

Chapter XII.

DADDY BY DEFAULT

The prospect of being a father can be an intimidating event for any man. So imagine being a ten or eleven year old boy; or even younger in some cases, being told that you are the man of the house. Picture having younger brothers or sisters who come to you declaring they are hungry and your mother has spent all of the family's money on drugs or alcohol. Either daddy was never there or maybe one day he decided that he did not want to be a daddy anymore, leaving your mother for what he considers *"greener pastures"*. Now expand that situation even further and imagine the electric or gas is turned off or your mother has received a disconnection notice. She comes to you expressing that she needs your help with paying the bills, or even the rent.

How does a young boy respond to these situations? He cannot say *"no"*, but does not have skills that will translate into money. So how will he make a significant contribution to the household? There are only a few ways to make money with limited skills and most of them are illegal. Whether it involves selling drugs, committing thefts, or even selling their bodies, young men, children, are being asked to become *"daddies"* by default.

Every day in our society, children are being put into adult situations by being asked to make grown up decisions. In many cases, these kids are putting their educations as well as their freedom in jeopardy. In evaluating the options, many times selling drugs usually wins out because money can be made quickly in substantial amounts and the child's age does not matter. Unbeknownst to these young people is the fact that early decisions can significantly alter the direction of their lives. By pushing them into a *motive* situation it can be difficult for young men who find themselves being *"daddies by default"*, to alter their circumstances and change their *motive* into a *motivation*.

If it becomes *"necessary"* for a child to establish a hustle, such as selling drugs or other illegal behavior, there usually comes a time when the *"necessity"* of engaging in this extremely negative activity ends. There are those who have made significant amounts of money due to unlawful dealings. Once the original *motive* for becoming involved in their hustle ends, some individuals will quit their illegal *"work"*, using the money to invest in legal enterprises, others will continue hustling because they have become accustomed to ill-gotten gains or they feel trapped in *"the game"*.

Believe me, I am not one to knock someone else's hustle. The thing about hustling is that there are legal hustles and there are illegal hustles. I can't knock a positive legal hustle, in fact everyday is a hustle for most of us. However, I do not condone illegal activity in order to achieve a goal. A person may believe he *"has to do what he has to do"*, illegal or otherwise, in order to survive. Many of them are good people who have found themselves in bad situations, like being forced to make adult decisions as children. By the same token there are still those who take advantage of others just for the thrill of it.

For those good people, desperation may lead them to do wrong, especially if that is what he (or she) believes they must do in order to survive. I may not approve of some of the methods that are used, but I do understand how people end up in this position. This goes back to the point I made earlier when I addressed the issue of jail causing so many fathers to be out of their children's lives. If you are currently committing crimes in order to support your struggling family, it is still illegal and there is no question that you can end up in jail or worse, dead.

Just keep in mind that jails today are filled with people with good intentions who chose the wrong method to reach their objective. Thus, the *motivation* to provide for one's family morphs into a *motive* when negative methods are used to accomplish positive goals. Just as in math, a positive number multiplied by a negative number equals a negative number.

Good intentions tainted by negative actions results in negative outcomes. You do the math, it just does not add up. There is an old saying that *"the road to hell is paved with good intentions"*.

I am not attempting to judge, nor am I making light of very difficult situations. If you find yourself in a position where you have to make a decision between legal and illegal methods to provide for your family, I recommend choosing the legal path, which admittedly is not always the easiest. In the end, choosing to do what is right will be more spiritually and emotionally rewarding and it won't cost you your freedom. Fortunately, for most of us who make mistakes, we're given second chances. The severity of the mistakes will determine if another opportunity will be granted. So if you are thrust into the position of *"daddy by default"* just remember your overall objective is your family and those who really need you. Don't do something foolish that will jeopardize your freedom or your life.

Chapter XIII.

THE WORLD OWES ME SOMETHING

A sense of entitlement can create a great deal of frustration and pain. It can also lead to disappointing yourself and others. In our *"right now"* generation filled with tangible things and empty promises, it is possible that a *daddiless* child feels like the world owes him or her something. Some *daddiless* children have a perception that since their daddy was taken away from them, whether he walked away, went to jail, abused drugs, or even died, everybody owes them something. Whether it was the toys they did not receive as a child or the clothes that they never had, there can be a sense that they deserve those things one way or another. Even if it means taking what they want from someone else or taking advantage of others. *"Entitled"* individuals will sometimes resort to crime to get what they want.

Most people who have a strong work ethic believe it is necessary to labor and put an effort forth in order to attain all they want in life. Nevertheless, there are those who allow the *motive* of being without, due to their *daddilessness*, to push them to steal, kill, and destroy in order to obtain what they desire. For these selfish individuals it does not matter who gets hurt. All that matters (to them) is that they get what they want, when they want it.

If a person goes through life believing that others owe them something it is much easier to justify stealing. Maybe this is how people rationalize committing crimes like robbery or burglary, which involves taking other people's property. These individuals' logic is drastically flawed because they believe they are just recovering what is already theirs. Their victims have worked and sacrificed for what they acquired. However, thieves feel secure in believing they do not have to put forth the same effort in order to receive the same reward. The real tragedy is that the offenders do not feel remorse about stealing valuables from others who may have worked years to obtain this property.

It is important to understand that idol possessions will not fill the hole in your soul; therefore, it is useless to attempt to replace the absence of your father's love with tangible things. Besides, the victims of these crimes are not to blame for the perpetrator's circumstances. Why must the innocent suffer? Maybe it is sheer vindictiveness or hatred for people who have all of the things that the wrongdoers wanted growing up. The reality is their past cannot be changed; they can only work toward a better future, but *"hating on"* others because of their success is really another symptom of self-hatred. When a person does not like their self, there is a lack of concern and remorse for others. The feeling of selfishness that's associated with taking from others has to be a manifestation of the pain these individuals feel. It is almost as if they are desensitized or numb and have no regard for other people's feelings. These folks are only concerned with their personal satisfaction. This sounds ironically similar to the way their fathers seemed to feel about them. Thus, this thievery appears to be a perpetuation of the negative experiences these people have gone through in their lives. My mother used to say *"two wrongs don't make a right"* and her words could not be truer, especially in these circumstances. Making others feel pain just because you want others to experience how you feel is just cruel. The wrong that was caused by their father's absence should not be the justification for doing wrong to others.

A person has to be on a serious ego trip when he or she builds their self up to be more necessary than everyone else. This is not to say that a person should consider him or herself to be less important than anyone else, but that does not mean another person should be devalued and considered insignificant just to build yourself up. The *daddiless* child who walks around with a chip on his or her shoulder is in for a rude awakening if they believe society owes them something. In many ways, these children are setting themselves up for disappointment if they believe others will view their circumstances the same way they do. Since *daddiless* situations are so commonplace, many people are not fazed or even concerned when they hear about these situations, unless something extreme happens. In a lot of instances, the only time these *daddiless* children get the attention of others is when crime occurs (robberies, assaults, murder, etc.). The crimes will generally get the public's attention, at least briefly. It is shameful that it takes something so severe before people will take notice of these heartbroken children.

In looking at the other end of the spectrum, there are those who do not steal, but they are always looking for a *"hand out"*. As opposed to being thieves, these children are extremely needy and in some situations unjustifiably so. The rationale from their perspective is that there is no need to work because others will take care of them. Many times these children look to other family members to provide them with what they want and need. Even after they reach adulthood, they never become self-sufficient and are dependent on their mothers, the welfare system or others to take care of them. Again, there is a belief that everyone else owes them something so they must take care of them. Some mothers continue to provide for their adult children because they feel guilty that they could not give them *"things"* when they were younger. The mothers are doing their children a greater disservice by not allowing them to exercise independence. In the end, these children may rely on others for the rest of their lives.

Personally, I have come to realize that nothing in life is promised. Nothing is guaranteed, except death. No one owes any of us anything, but we owe it to ourselves to be the best that we can be and to overcome our circumstances. No one should care more about improving your situation than you do. The fundamental aspect to grasp is that you have a GOD given gift inside and it should not be used to do wrong. This gift is given freely and does not have to be taken. It's already yours. Once you open up your mind and decide to use it, your gift will make room for you.

Chapter XIV.

IDENTITY CRISIS

Knowing who you are as a person is so important to your psychological well-being; without this knowledge, you may go through your life aimlessly. There is really no way to determine how your sense of identity is affected by the absence of your father. For me personally, there was a time in my life when I wondered to myself, *"Where do I fit in?"* I would not consider myself introverted or inhibited by any stretch of the imagination; but I am reserved around people I do not know and sometimes even around people I do know. That is because trusting people and feeling as if I was a part of their circle was difficult. In many instances, I felt like an outsider.

Growing up the way I did, with the hand me down clothes and a lack of money, our circles were not large. Most of my childhood friends had lives very similar to mine; we were poor, struggling, and *daddiless*. Some of them had a little more than others, maybe a washing machine (so their clothes were not as dirty), or a *"beat up"* car to get around in, but for the most part, we were all similarly situated.

People can be harsh when you are a *"have not."* They would laugh at the holes in our clothes or the fact that we were wearing the same clothes more than once during a given week.

As a result of feeling humiliated, when I encountered individuals who were outside of my environment I was always apprehensive and concerned about being rejected. After feeling denied by my father I was leery about trusting many others. I never had the nicest clothes or the newest sneakers, not even in college, so I was always self-conscious about whether or not I was acceptable. Even in high school, I knew there were girls who thought I was cute, but none of them would want to be seen with the kid with only one pair of jeans.

When I attended college things did not change much, at least not during the early years. My clothes did not change much either. I remember I had a pair of white sandals that I would wear quite often. When I bought them in August I was getting ready for college. I considered them my *"dress shoes"* because I did not have any others. I would wear them anytime I needed to be *"dressed up"* or wear a tie. After the last few days of August had come and gone and fall was setting in, the shoes were no longer appropriate; they were vented and air would flow right through them. As the months began to pass and the days became colder, I was still wearing these summer shoes. Once the snow was on the ground, there was no way I should have been wearing these shoes, but I did. To make matters worse, I wore them so much a hole formed in the sole of one of the shoes. Moreover, the shoes were very cheap and the soles were not leather nor rubber; they were made of some kind of weird foam material. The material eroded quickly, especially when I scraped my foot on the ground, as I occasionally did. Not too many people knew it, but throughout my first semester of college, I walked through the snow with a hole in my shoe, freezing!

My foolish logic and pride allowed me to believe that since I did not have any dress shoes, I was better off wearing the *"dressy"* sandals instead of wearing sneakers with dress pants. Looking back on this, my dirty old sneakers would not have looked any sillier than those shoes looked and I would have been a lot warmer. Considering I wore tube socks with the sandals anyway, what would have been the difference?

For the longest time, I was chasing acceptance. My personality and character were intact because of how my mother raised me, but I was constantly seeking the approval of others. I never took this desire for acceptance to any extreme. For some *daddiless* children the desire for acceptance is a *motive* for making poor choices and doing things that do not enhance their character. Peer pressure can be very destructive if a person allows it to be. People have been known to steal, kill, and manipulate just to be liked. Nice children can be mean; non-drinkers and non-drug users can be *"pushed"* to drink or abuse drugs; peaceful people can be *"forced"* to fight, and the list goes on and on.

In spite of my own insecurities, I have never been one to put myself into a box. I have always been able to enter into any environment and interact. My ability to adapt and be comfortable ranges from the courtroom to the poolroom; I can go into either space and represent very well. I must say that my ability to adapt is truly a gift from GOD. Here I am, a kid from the ghetto with no background in public speaking or experience in the courtroom, and I can go in and articulate my client's position extremely well. At the same time, I can go out and shoot craps with the fellas or play spades with my friends without feeling out of place.

My ability to go from *"suit"* to *"street"*, so to speak, was always an advantage for me as a criminal defense lawyer. I could talk to my clients, relate to them and understand them, but at the same time, I could speak to the court in an eloquent manner that was respectful and well received. I call this being able to *"flip the script"* and it works. Most people have their professional *"at work voice"* and then there is their social *"hanging out with your friends voice"*. Being diverse is absolutely necessary in order to be successful in life and in business. You cannot embrace just one way of thinking and believe you will achieve everything that life has to offer. The thing about an identity crisis is people begin to wonder which characteristics best represent who they are. Can you truly be yourself or do you have to fake it to make it?

Regardless of not having a strong relationship with my father, I continue to maintain solid and lasting friendships. At times, I have experienced difficulty in socializing. In some instances, I even felt disconnected or uncomfortable, especially in new and unfamiliar surroundings. It was difficult for me to stay engaged, even with some of the most interesting people. Maybe it was my own personal attention deficit disorder, but (sometimes) when I was genuinely interested in what someone was saying, I would find myself drifting, struggling to stay focused. I do not believe I was so self-centered and superficial that I only wanted to talk about myself; it was just difficult feeling connected. In order to feel linked to others you need to relate to them. I found it complicated to understand someone or something I knew nothing about. Further, there was the issue of trust. Trust is necessary to feel connected to others; and that was not something that I was going to give up easily.

As *daddiless* children, we learn to guard our hearts and feelings, so it requires more than a superficial relationship for us to truly be engaged. Unless I was with very close friends or family I would feel self-conscious, wondering how other people perceived me. Did I qualify as an intellectual or was I still being viewed as the poor boy from the ghetto? As I have grown, I have frequently asked myself what surroundings are best suited for me? I am no longer poor so I do not spend as much time around people who are in financial need; however, I do not feel comfortable around *"high and mighty"* folks either. I would say I enjoy being around people that are somewhere in the middle. I can actually relate to both individuals that have earned formal educations as well as those who have not. I have street knowledge in addition to book knowledge and I am a product of both environments. Never forgetting where I came from helps me to stay grounded and to not be critical of those who are still there. It is interesting that whenever I tell people I grew up in the projects many of them find it hard to believe. They express their disbelief by saying, *"you could not have grown up in the hood"*. My response is, *"you can't judge a book by its cover"*. Is it so unbelievable that I grew up in a single parent household, in adverse circumstances, but was able to overcome and get an education? It took a lot of hard work and dedication, but I did it.

The ironic thing is that I did not learn to speak well or articulate in school; I learned this skill from watching television and listening to the dialogue. I learned slang from the streets, but I learned to adapt from experience. My formal education and my street wisdom seemed to compete against one another, which continued to add to my identity crisis. Which group could I relate to the most, my old friends from the neighborhood or my college friends?

Although I am friendly, polite, respectful, and fun, at times I feel as if my social skills are lacking. When I considered the identity dynamic, one factor most of my friends and I had in common was we were raised primarily by our mothers. In my opinion, it is necessary to have an equal amount of participation from both your mother and father in order to help a child develop and establish appropriate social skills. I believe this involvement will help to create balance for the child and helps to produce a stable individual.

As far as my social skills, I really believe I have a lot to offer anyone that I consider my friend. When I know a person and I am comfortable around them, I do not have a problem with being myself in their presence. However, I do not feel it is necessary to be guarded once a person has gained my trust. My friends are non-judgmental and they like me just as I am. Additionally, there is a commonality between our social circles and how we were raised. Many of my closest friends grew up the same way I did. Two of my best friends grew up with almost identical circumstances as mine; we were all poor and *daddiless*. My other best friend had both his parents present, but there was such an age disparity between him and his father that it was hard for the two of them to relate to one another. Thus, all of us were raised primarily by our mothers.

I also learned that most individuals tend to gravitate toward people with whom they have something in common. If the element that links them together is the fact that they are *daddiless,* will it mean these children will mainly associate with other *daddiless* people? The next question is how do they view their *daddiless* situation, is it a *"motive"* or a *"motivation?"* It really matters how the *daddiless* people you associate with view their situations. Are they seeing life without their father in a positive or negative way? How does this mindset translate into their perception of the world and their attitudes? Then the question becomes are you a follower or are you a leader? If you are running with those who look at *daddilessness* as a *motive* to do wrong, are you allowing them to influence you to do wrong? Do you look at life as limitless or are you bound up by what you do not have?

If you decide to associate with people who perceive their *daddilessness* as a *motive* to behave poorly, then negativity can run rampant and you may find yourself constantly in trouble. Thinking this way may also lead one to being involved in crime and hanging out in negative places with negative people. Many of these individuals are not family oriented and this can result in a continuation of *"daddilessness"*. If you surround yourself with negative viewpoints about family, this is more likely to influence your attitude and possibly affect your belief system. The old saying *"birds of a feather flock together"* comes to mind.

Alternatively, if you do not allow your *daddilessness* to taint your outlook on things you will attract other *daddiless* people that are equally committed to positivity and family, sometimes more committed than those who grew up with both parents. We, fatherless children, know what we lacked growing up and there is an extremely strong desire to establish the relationships that we did not have.

Fortunately, I was able to find friends who maintain a great sense of family despite being *daddiless*. All of us are dedicated to maintaining strong, loving relationships with our children and families. I believe these attitudes were greatly influenced by the relationships we had with positive male figures. Our grandfathers, brothers, uncles, cousins, and family friends have served as role models whom we look to for guidance. These men have assisted us with establishing strong foundations built around family by showing us what family should look like. Positive male examples provided direction and helped play an important role in shaping our views about family and life.

Social skills are taught. Observations and interactions can be some of the best ways for individuals to learn how to relate to one another. Many people learn how to interact with the opposite sex or their peers by reflecting on the things they have seen their parents do. If one parent is missing, it can leave a void in the development of the child. If a person is not shown how to handle themselves in social situations there can be confusion about what is appropriate or inappropriate behavior. As I indicated previously, a mother can only teach a boy so much about certain male practices; the same is true for a father attempting to teach his daughter. In some instances, experience is a great teacher. Sometimes it is necessary to experience certain situations in order to know how to deal with them.

By and large, parents are the ones who assist their children with their self-esteem at an early age. Parental reinforcement helps to build a child's confidence to face whatever social challenges they may encounter. For example, a father's involvement in his little girl's life can reinforce her belief that she is beautiful and should be treated with dignity and respect by boys. This encouragement may prevent her from being manipulated or taken advantage of by guys who use compliments as a means to influence her. Without these compliments from her father, she may be vulnerable to "*smooth talkers*" who do not have her best interest at heart.

For young boys, a father can build his son's confidence by showing him how to be strong and assertive when necessary. He can show his son how to treat a young lady based upon how he treats the boy's mother. When a child has an opportunity to see how their mother and father interact it provides them positive examples of what is and is not acceptable. Leading by example and speaking positivity into a child's life will definitely build up his or her self-esteem and assist them with their ability to communicate and interact in social settings.

The best way to overcome this identity crisis is to change your image of yourself. Some "*daddiless*" children tend to lack self-confidence and in many ways have a sense of self-hatred that can propel them into destructive behavior. One of the best ways to overcome this lack of confidence is being surrounded by confident people and removing negative influences from your life. When I suggest surrounding yourself with confident people, I want to clarify that it should be individuals who are secure in themselves and do not feel the need to put you down in order to assert their own self-esteem.

Do not allow yourself to be intimidated by other people's self-assurance. A shift in mindset will allow you to operate in the security of who you are and what you have to offer the world. With a change of thinking, you will begin to adapt to almost any environment. Speak positivity into your life as well. Make self-affirming comments and say them aloud to yourself. Declaring negative outcomes becomes a self-fulfilling prophecy. If you say you will not be able to accomplish a goal, more than likely, you will not. Over the years, I have dealt with my own personal identity crisis. In addressing my situation, I have learned I do not have to choose which characteristics are best for me because all of them are what make me the person that I am. Your destiny is really up to you.

I realize some things are easier said than done, but if you change your thinking, you can change your life. Give yourself a chance to create the life that you want with the people you want to be around. Do not allow your missing daddy to stop you from getting to know yourself.

Chapter XV.

I'M A MAN

As a man, I can speak to the fact that many of us strive to be independent. While it is true that neither men nor woman appreciate being told what to do; this is particularly prevalent with men. Boys are taught to be strong and to hold their ground to prevent others from pushing them around. This behavior is commonly perceived as stubbornness, but for many men this behavior exemplifies masculinity. So when is it that a man, a real man, feels the need to proclaim he's a man? Most of the time it is either when he is not behaving like a man or someone is challenging his manhood.

So, exactly what defines a man? Clearly, it is not announcing you're a man. In many instances, these statements are actually more of an opinion as opposed to a foregone conclusion. The interpretation of some men as to what constitutes being a man is based upon a number of misguided ideas. Some guys believe the number of sexual conquests they've had with women, the number of children they fathered outside of wedlock, their ability to fistfight, or how much respect they garnered on the streets; are the attributes that make them men. If a father believes that these things make him a man then he is more likely to leave his children; he is self centered and not really concerned with anyone or anything else.

These ideas are destructive and are truly an extension of the *daddiless* problem. Some of these behaviors, such as being a womanizer, a brawler, or a hustler can even lead to death. Regrettably, many individuals are brought up believing these erroneous ideas because they did not have their fathers around as male role models to demonstrate how a real man should carry on. Some guys have learned their ways from street hustlers and *"players"* who modeled negative behavior they observed over the years. In many cases, the *"role models"* did not care anything about their protégé's well-being; as a result, they fed them selfish and destructive information. A responsible and caring dad would not deceive his child by allowing him or her to go down a harmful and irresponsible path. While there are hustlers that will steer a young man clear of their ways in an attempt to guide them down the right path, life on the streets is generally not one that begets love and nurturing. Quite the contrary, ruthless and scandalous behaviors are the norms.

Oddly enough, when I was younger, I personally had a drug dealing pimp help to steer me in the right direction. Ironically, he was a nice, kind-hearted person. He worked in the grocery store around the corner from the projects where we lived. He actually lived in the projects too. In those days, he seemed really cool. He had fancy cars and nice clothes along with lots of pretty women. I was probably seven or eight years old when I met him. We met via his niece, a beautiful girl who had a lot of personality. Her nickname was Panda. Panda's mother was a prostitute who walked around the ghetto with fur fox stoles and mink coats. Panda also had nice things. At the time, I had no idea that her mother was a prostitute, but as I grew up it became very obvious what she did for a living. Different men were always coming to their apartment to pick her up and she always seemed to have money.

Panda's family members were some of the nicest people you would ever meet. Her mother, grandmother, aunt and uncle would all give me money. Panda's grandmother would send me to the grocery store with pop bottles. In those days, you could take an eight pack of glass soda bottles back to the store to obtain a ten-cent deposit on each bottle. When she sent me to the store to buy another eight pack she would give me the change from the deposit along with another dollar for myself. Since we did not have very much money in our household I could always buy myself candy or food with the change I earned.

Panda's uncle was as cool as a fan. He would always talk to me about positive things and encourage me to stay in school. He would always ask me about my grades and if I was regularly attending school. His interest in what was going on in my life really meant a lot. I guess he could see that I was a good kid who was not into all of the bad behaviors other kids were getting into.

The thing I remember most about him was his car; he had a shiny gold Pontiac Trans Am with a huge firebird on the hood. That was my dream car in those days. I think it was because of the movie *"Smokie and the Bandit"* starring Burt Reynolds. Her uncle's car had T-tops and everything just like the one in the movie. I thought he was the coolest guy in the city. I would tell him that when I grew up I wanted a car like his. He told me that if I worked hard and stayed in school I could have anything that I wanted. I found out later that he had been selling drugs out of the grocery store where he worked. Despite his choice of *"professions"*, he apparently had a caring heart, at least for me.

The main reason that I brought up Panda and her Uncle was to emphasize the fact that *motivation* can come from anywhere and examples of manhood can come from some of the most peculiar places. Moreover, I want to highlight that even when a man makes poor choices, he can still impart positive wisdom. It's important that people recognize that even if a man does bad things, he may still have good intentions. Most individuals involved in a criminal lifestyle would not recommend or encourage others to live that way.

From my point of view, a man is defined by how he handles adversity and responds to a challenge. Does he crumble under pressure or does he rise to the occasion? In many instances, the act of being a father is truly one of those defining moments that help a man establish his manhood. But not all men end up having children and I'm not saying that all men should. However, if the situation requires that a man take on that responsibility, he should not run from it; he should embrace it.

Let's look at how some men decide to prove their manhood. First and foremost, if a boy grows up without any guidance or instruction on what it takes to be a man he is more likely to attempt to make his own way. That may result in some misguided ways of establishing that he's a man. In the constant struggle for acceptance from their peers, as well as the opposite sex, many young men can become susceptible to bad influences. Without examples of how to interact with other men or how to impress a girl, a young man may do some extreme things in order to get respect or establish himself.

The term "respect" and "disrespect" becomes a major focus for some young men. These terms are thrown around all the time. In the black community, respect has been something that has been fought for and sought after for many years. People have been killed for acts of alleged disrespect. The search for respect is somewhat distorted in the black community, primarily because of our legacy of being treated as less than human during slavery. Once some degree of respect was earned there was no willingness to compromise in that area at all. For example, after so many years of being called *"boy"*, regardless of age, black men began to refer to one another as *"man"*. This is now a term of endearment and was purposefully done in order to avoid the disrespectful acts of those who attempted to oppress them. Simple things like recognizing one another in a considerate way, even when others did not, is just one of the methods that black men began to adapt to ensure they obtained respect even when others tried to deny them of it. Therefore, nowadays, even the slightest feeling of disrespect is not ignored by most boys or men and can lead to serious negative situations.

For most men respect is extremely important and is one of the primary attributes sought by many to show they have achieved manhood. So how do you gain respect? Among the men I know, respect is not just given, it is earned. In many cases, how you earn respect depends upon your environment. For example, when you are in the streets, respect (or what is perceived as respect) is gained from your street reputation. On the streets, respect is usually based upon fear or intimidation. The more people that are afraid or intimidated by an individual the more respect he or she has in the streets. In the business world, respect is associated with status. Status is based upon how much money a person has, the school they went to, the people they have influence over, or the material things they have acquired. All of these examples are worldly reflections of power and control, which translates into respect.

It becomes obvious that a misguided boy will grow up to be a misguided man if no positive influences come into play to change his thinking. In many ways, it's easy to be responsible for yourself, but when you become a father you become responsible for someone else. Thus, avoiding the responsibility of being a father is, in many ways, really avoiding being a man.

Chapter XVI.

DYSFUNCTION AND DISCONNECTION

In some situations, *daddilessness* can occur even if a father is present in the household. These fathers are physically present, but emotionally detached. It is similar to being in a crowded room, but still feeling alone. How many times do you think that the feeling of being alone is amplified when you arrive home from school every day and your mom and dad barely speak to one another, or dare to engage you in conversation? To compound the situation, each family member spends their time in different rooms of the house, which prevents quality interaction with one another.

What happens when an attention starved child desires to be noticed and acknowledged? What happens to a girl who finally is showered with attention from a boy? What if he does not really have her best interest at heart? What if there are multiple boys? Alternatively, what occurs when an attention-starved boy catches the eye of a girl and he has the wrong intentions? When there is no male role model for these children to pattern themselves after, they will emulate what they see on television or try to do things independently. Many times, these children's choices are clouded by hormones. In the absence of solid values, decision-making can be based upon unsound principles. In certain cases, the feelings of emptiness and the lack of solid examples become the perfect storm (or the perfect recipe) for disaster.

For many girls and women, even if their fathers are in their lives, it may be difficult for these men to get through the awkwardness of dealing with their daughter's female issues. Many times the father will defer to the child's mother to handle those situations. Since these fathers don't deal with their wives, there is no wonder he doesn't know how to address his daughter. Other fathers do not know how to interact with their daughters in a way that makes them feel loved. When a girl does not have positive examples from her father to show how she should be treated by other males, this may leave her susceptible to accepting substandard treatment. Not all men know how to model open communication with their children and this may result in superficial discussions that lack much substance. When he feels uncomfortable about a particular issue, he is more likely to avoid it and leave the child to her own methods to discover the answers. As a result, when these children have problems they are reluctant to share them with their fathers. Either way, the opportunity is lost for him to connect and share his wisdom with his child.

For young women the issue is compounded even more because disrespect and disconnection becomes her norm; it's what she comes to expect when she interacts with men because she was not exposed to anything different. Therefore, when and if she enters into a relationship she does not have high expectations of how she should be treated. This can result in toxic interactions for her. She may date various men, but she may never establish a committed relationship because she never learned to trust men. Thus, her father's inability to connect with her on an emotional level becomes the *motive*, continuing this negative cycle all over again.

For some young people the generational curses I spoke about earlier tend to manifest themselves. Sexual promiscuity usually becomes the norm when young women are seeking love in the wrong places. Some girls can become indiscriminate about their sexual partners. This behavior can result in a girl having a reputation that no young woman wants. Once this happens, her self-esteem is damaged even more. She may begin to take on an *"I don't care attitude"*. She begins to believe that what she does will not matter and her character is irreparably tainted; so she continues to be *"loose"*.

The young woman may not make much of an effort to change the perceptions that people have of her, whether they are right or wrong. In certain cases, being ashamed of past indiscretions can result in a downward spiral of more self-hatred as well as self-destructive behavior. The young girl may even turn to drugs or alcohol and possibly become addicted. The other thing about these girls using drugs and/or alcohol is that with the abuse comes a loss of inhibitions and the possibility of them becoming pregnant while intoxicated. As a consequence of this negative behavior the generational curse of *"daddilessness"* may be continued.

By no means am I advocating that a young girl has to work hard to change the perception that others have of her. People are going to believe what they want. It is best to avoid putting themselves in situations where other people have ammunition to make judgments about their character.

For other women, the impact of being disconnected from their fathers will cause them difficulty when trusting men. The women may be too bitter and angry to allow a *"good man"* to be a part of their lives. Some women tend to have an attraction to the wrong type of guys, men that will not treat them well. These relationships may consist of physical and emotional abuse. When a person operates out of pain instead of love so many negative consequences can occur. These women continue to have lingering questions about their fathers. Why is he rejecting me? Why does he ignore me? Why is he making me feel like I have done something wrong to him?

There are no definitive answers. It may be a situation where the father thought he was doing the right thing by marrying the child's mother when she got pregnant. Therefore, the two of them maintained a loveless marriage. Despite the fact that both parents thought they were doing the right thing, they end up doing more damage than good to the child. Alternatively, maybe he was never taught how to show his emotions, so when he got married, or began his relationship with the child's mother, he did not know how to interact as a husband or father should. Some men grow up without an emotional connection to their parents, which leads them to have the same disconnect with their own families. This is unfortunate, especially for little girls. Many girls learn how a man should treat them by watching their fathers interact with their mothers. Little girls want attention from their fathers. When girls are not noticed by their fathers they may seek to replace him by getting the attention of another *"father figure"*. In some cases, these *"father figures "* do not have the young woman's best interests at heart. Many times these older men end up molesting the girl or even getting her pregnant. All of these scenarios can stem from growing up in a dysfunctional and disconnected family unit.

These scenarios are examples of perpetual cycles that occur when a father does not communicate to his daughter what she should expect from a young man when he is dating her. Fathers can make their daughters aware of the types of games that men play to manipulate women. It really goes to show how important the role of a father is in a young girl's life. The sad part is that children look to their daddies as their protectors, especially when they feel insecure or afraid. So whether the father is physically or emotionally unavailable, what are the potential consequences of his absence? Most of the time solace will be sought in the arms of a guy who is willing to listen, even if it turns out to be a guy with flawed standards.

The flip side to this situation is that some of these young ladies are able to use their dysfunctional circumstances as a *"motivation"*. When this happens, the children strive to excel. Many children become overachievers, straight "A" students, members of honor societies, and active in organizations. The children use these actions partly to obtain the attention and approval of their parents. Many times, despite these efforts, the child never really receives the acknowledgement he or she was seeking from the people they wanted it from the most. Other children learn that the focus is placed on them when they engage in negative behavior such as committing crimes, partaking of alcohol and drugs, self-mutilating, attempting suicide, or even homicide.

Subconsciously, these children are actually crying out for acknowledgement and acceptance. Regrettably, they have come to believe that the only way they can get the attention they seek will be to participate in damaging and destructive behavior. If you find yourself fitting the description of the fathers I just described, I hope you begin to acknowledge your role. Do not continue to ignore your children. The results of your failure to interact can be devastating. Take the time to listen and provide the advice your children may need to help them resolve their issues because if you don't someone else will.

Chapter XVII.

WHAT IF THEY'RE BOTH GONE

Today, probably more than ever, grandparents and other family members are raising children that are not their own. This is the result of a sister, brother, son or daughter walking out on their responsibilities and leaving another family member to raise their child or children. In most cases, the family members feel as if they have no other option than to take the child into their home to prevent him or her from growing up in foster care. While this is not their child, he or she is their flesh and blood so there is no way they are going to let this child grow up with strangers.

This is quite the predicament when a family member takes on the responsibility of raising a child that's not theirs. The family members will have to deal with the psychological affects that go along with raising a child who doesn't have the nurturing of either parent. The *"new parents"* will be the ones who hear the child crying himself or herself to sleep at night and saying how much he or she misses mommy or daddy. The situation must be extremely difficult because the person who is causing the children pain is their family member and the person feeling the pain is as well. Depending on the circumstances, these types of issues can absolutely divide a family.

In addition to the emotional aspects of raising a family member's child, there is the financial component. If a relative decides to get a court order that gives them temporary custody of the child, the county or state will provide very little or no financial assistance to care for the child, especially if the family member earns over a certain amount of money. In a cruel twist of fate and despite their good intentions, assisting their family member places some individuals in precarious financial circumstances. Caring for the child will result in various expenses being created or increased. Things like, food, clothing, day care, after school care, and medical costs for these children are all new expenses that are borne by their unexpected family members. If they have children of their own this can place a heavy emotional burden on the nuclear family members as well and it can ultimately influence the relationship these parents have with their kids.

Furthermore, consider what effect this arrangement can have on a marriage. How will the spouse and technically the non-blood relative deal with having the responsibility of caring for this child? Even some of the strongest relationships can be strained when attention and money have to be split. The selfish decision by the child's parents can have far-reaching effects on many other people. When the child's parents left, they probably did not consider all of the repercussions their absences would create, and if they did, they probably did not care.

Now consider the grandparents who are raising their children's child or children. They have already done their job of rearing children. However, they are put back into a situation of raising an infant, toddler, preteen, or teenager during a time that is meant to be their golden years. They do not have the opportunity to spend time enjoying their grandchildren and then having the luxury of sending them home to their parents after the visit. In many cases, they are on a fixed income or have just enough for themselves, but are now expected to provide financially for their grandchild. Why do they do it? Maybe they do not want their grandchild growing up in foster care. Others may blame themselves for the shortcomings of their children and they think it may have been something that they did or did not do that caused their child to abandon their own offspring.

In the absence of a child's parents, the roles of other family members get out of order. Grandma and granddad become mommy-grandma and daddy-granddad, respectively. Aunts or uncles do not have the ability to just be aunts or uncles, but serve the dual roles of mama-auntie or daddy-uncle. Stepping in to raise someone else's child can potentially cause resentment toward the irresponsible family member and, in many cases, the child as well. The resentment for the child can be an unfortunate consequence of the whole matter but no one wants to feel like they don't have a choice in a situation. The family members feel like they really do not have another option but to help as they contemplate the potential outcome to the child if they do not help out. It is one thing when a child's parent dies and other family members are needed to care for him or her. However, it is completely different when a physically capable and mentally stable individual chooses to leave his or her child. The parents' infrequent visits and the constant movement in and out of their child's life (at their leisure) can definitely result in anger, hostility and bitterness.

It may be heartbreaking for a child not to have its father, in my opinion, it is so much more impactful and hurtful for a mother to leave her child. Feelings of being unwanted are amplified a hundred fold when the child's mother leaves. Why is this my opinion? Well, in most situations, a mother's love is deemed unconditional. Mothers will usually do whatever they can for their child(ren). Generally, it is unimaginable for a mother to leave her child. Think about it, whenever you see an athlete on television or an entertainer getting an award, you hear them say, *"Hi mom"* or *"I want to dedicate this award to my mother."* Most of the time you will hear a mother get recognition well in advance of hearing an acknowledgement of a father. This is mainly because of the bond between a mother and her child. When this connection is never fully formed or breaks down it can be extremely damaging for the child.

It would seem that mothers would have more of an attachment to their offspring as they have carried their children for nine months while pregnant. The mother and child are literally bonded to one another from the very beginning by the umbilical cord. Thus, she does not have the ability to just get up and leave at her leisure. Conversely, the father does not have the same type of connection. His body is not necessary for the survival of the child and this leaves him with the option to come and go when he wants. Thus, it may be much easier for him to walk away before the child is born. Based upon the link between the mother and the child, one would logically conclude that it would be much more difficult for a mother to part with her kids.

If both parents are gone, it would appear to be even more difficult for the child to overcome their circumstances and avoid having these absences become a *motive* instead of a *motivation*. These children are dealing with the fact that the two people in this world who were supposed to love, care for, mold, and protect them have abandoned him or her. These children are technically being told that they need to fend for themselves because if a family member does not step up, the state is expected to care for the child, which translates into the child being an orphan.

For a child to deal with not having the love or guidance of either parent would appear to be a *"double whammy"* unless there are strong and well-grounded family members to help the child adapt and cope with the circumstances. Even if there are strong grandparents, aunts, and uncles in the child's life to show them what family and love are supposed to look like, the emotional scars of being rejected by their mother and father will take time to heal. I know of a young man who has been subjected to the *"loss"* of both his parents. No, they are not deceased, as the word *"loss"* tends to indicate. These parents choose not to be actively involved in his life. His mother floats in and out of his life without a lot of consistency or stability. It is unfortunate when a mother or father decides to play parent when it is convenient for them. It is even more regrettable that they cannot be relied upon to finance or at least assist with their child's needs. Additionally, there is the feeling of pain and disappointment that the child must feel when realizing he or she cannot depend on their parents because they are unreliable.

There are only so many broken promises and missed birthdays that children can endure before they are prone to distrust everyone else because of the inactions with their parents. From my perspective, the act of running back and forth in and out of the child's life does more damage to them than not having their parents there at all. I believe this to be true because it is like being teased with something that you want more than anything. It seems like torment when a relationship is right there in their grasp and then repeatedly snatched away. In many ways, it is comparable to creating false hope that the parent will be with them and then pulling the rug right out from under them. This dangling of parental love in the child's face will most definitely hurt more than not having this occur at all.

It has been said, *"it's better to have loved and to have lost than to never had love at all."* When it comes to the on again, off again love of a parent, I must say I disagree. Unless the child works to repair the lack of trust that is created by this relationship, it can affect many other associations that the child will have in future. I'm sure it will be extremely difficult for a child to trust anyone if he or she cannot fully rely on their own mother and father. In many ways, this on again off again relationship actually has a benefit because the child will have actual firsthand knowledge that their parent is a liar as opposed to it being hearsay. It is one thing to think that someone does not operate with integrity, it is quite another to know it for a fact. This could result in the child resenting his parent more in the long-run. I personally believe it is better to know the type of person that you are dealing with as opposed to being mislead for an extended period. Unless the parent is committed to being a consistent and meaningful part of the child's life, he or she may prefer that the mother or father just stay away.

Chapter XVIII.

IT'S LIKE HE WAS DEAD TO ME

Being *daddiless* can incite a great number of emotions. One of the most prevalent feelings that *daddiless* children exhibited is anger. As a means of coping with their anger, some children have found it easier to think of their fathers as being *"dead"*. Before I met my father, it was as if he was dead to me. Maybe even more than that, I felt like he did not even exist. I had no faith in the idea that I had a father. The bible tells us *"faith is the substance of things hoped for and the evidence of things not seen."* Well, I had hoped for a daddy but there was no evidence that he really existed. People would tell me that they knew my father. I even had individuals come to me and tell me they were related to me on my father's side. It was like my father was this mythological figure that I heard about, but had never seen. In my mind and heart, this man could have been anyone or no one, I did not care which.

Thinking of someone as being dead when they are not may seem like an extreme way of handling a painful situation. The thing is, considering him deceased is sometimes less painful because it gives a child some degree of comfort to know he is not able to spend time with them as opposed to being unwilling. The reality of *"believing"* one's parent is dead, either real or imagined, can be a *motive* or a *motivation*.

One of the most heartbreaking things that I have experienced in my life was the death of my first cousin. According to all reports, he was in the best shape of his life, unexpectedly he passed away from what appeared to be a heart attack; he was thirty-five! My cousin was a wonderful person with a spectacular personality and a spirit for helping others, especially children. I think the situation was so impactful because he was like a brother to me. His mother and father became my surrogate parents. I would spend as many weekends as I could at their house. It was my place of respite and peace. They showed me what marriage and a family was supposed to look like. Therefore, with his death, I lost the little brother that I never had. The other thing about his death that hurt so much was how close we were in age and the fact that he had two young children, ages eight and six, who are going to have to grow up without their *"daddy"*. I want to emphasize the fact that my cousin was a *"daddy"*, not just a *"father"*.

A real death as opposed to an imagined one may still have the same effect. The pain associated with the absence of a child's father is repeated almost every time a situation occurs that would require his presence or participation. Having to explain why he is never present or having to deal with the embarrassment of telling people you are *"daddiless"* can incite anger and hurt on a recurring basis. It is also somewhat easier for people to empathize with the child if their father has passed away as opposed to having abandoned them. For those who have never experienced being left behind, it may be difficult for them to imagine such an event occurring. Without this experience, there are those who cannot truly relate to the child's feelings. When a father chooses to leave it raises questions. Was there something wrong with him or is there something wrong with your family that made him so uncomfortable that he left? Additionally, if he left there may be questions about the mother and her promiscuity, especially if her children are by different men and are all *daddiless*. Either way, some people may prejudge you or your family and decide you are *"damaged goods"* because you come from a *"broken home"*. After so many years of teasing or embarrassment from judgmental people, it may not be very hard for a child to consider their father dead.

When a person dies there is a period of time when mourning will take place. The grieving process may last weeks or even years depending on the individual. For the *daddiless* child who has never known their father there may be no grieving phase, at least not in the traditional sense. The pain and sorrow that goes along with missing someone or wishing they were present may still exist for the *daddiless*, but in reality, it is hard to miss someone they have never known. The *daddiless* child's feelings are related to the emptiness that is created by not having a daddy, not any emotional connection that existed between the two of them. Anger is the paramount emotion exhibited by most *daddiless* people. The thing about anger is that underneath this emotion is the true feeling of unhappiness and hurt. Many *daddiless* people have difficulty showing their true emotions, so they mask their hurt by presenting anger toward others. This is simply another defense mechanism that we use to protect ourselves from being hurt again. But being angry at the world will never bring your daddy back.

For some, declaring that their father is dead provides them with a sense of closure. These individuals are not just laying their fathers to rest figuratively, but emotionally as well. If their father has passed away, there is no longer a need to look for him and he cannot hurt them emotionally any longer. Thus, these children are attempting to bury their pain and any evidence of his existence in the hole that was left behind by his absence. Keeping him and these feelings buried in that place of emptiness helps to avoid dealing with either. The problem with this approach is that these folks are not addressing how they feel; they are just evading their pain instead of dealing with it.

Closing the chapter and filling the hole in our souls that is left by his absence is one of the most difficult things that we face as *daddiless* children. *"Out of sight and out of mind"* may be the philosophy that some will take on by considering their fathers dead to them. I believe avoiding your feelings is providing him with too much power over you.

Regardless of whether there was an actual or imagined death of a father, the child must learn to cope. The mechanism used to help him or her adjust may be a determining factor in whether the *motive* or the *motivation* will win out. Using anger as your coping mechanism will most certainly lead to self-destruction or the destruction of others. That will mean the *motive* will win. On the other hand, looking beyond your anger and addressing your pain by discussing how you feel, using your frustration as a *motivation* to do better and be better will bring about the healing that you so desperately need. You will either spiral out of control or take hold of your destiny in a positive way. As with all things in life, there is a choice to be made. Will the grief the child feels be paralyzing, preventing him or her from living their life to the fullest, or will they look at the symbolic death of their father as an inspiration to action? Hopefully, it will be the latter and not the former; let his *"death"* either perceived or otherwise stir up the courage you possess and your desire to be a better person than he was. Let it ensure that you will be present for your children.

I believe there are other factors that can contribute to the way these situations of loss unfold. Yes, self-motivation is the primary factor, but a positive support system is also necessary. Family members who love and care for these *daddiless* children will help them overcome their grief. This will help them realize that a brighter day can and will come, by refusing to wallow in self-pity and rising out of the dark place to conquer the hurt, peace can materialize. Regarding a parent as physically departed in some cases gives the child a sense of control they never possessed. In those cases, they have never known their father, the child has never had any say in anything. Everyone else in the situation influenced the direction of the child's life, everyone except the child. Now the children can determine how they view their father, possibly feeling empowered by having this control. If their father is dead, the rejection stops, but unfortunately, the hurt remains.

Whether a child experiences an actual death or a fictitious one, the love and support of family, as well as close friends, will assist in transforming this potential *motive* into *motivation*.

Chapter XIV.

ON THE FRINGE

If you have ever played golf you know that the *"fringe"* is outside of where you really want to be. The fringe is close, but still not actually on point. You can try your best to hit the ball toward the hole but it can cost you greatly if you aim in the wrong direction and miss the mark.

I would have to say that my relationship with my father has been on the fringe. Over the years, we have tried to connect, but have not quite hit the mark. We have both made the effort and in some ways we have grown closer. Along the way, I have grown fond of him as a person. I have come to care about him and his well-being. However, he and I have not been able to solidify a *daddy* and son relationship. When I began writing this chapter I considered entitling it *"missed opportunities"*. I think that is the best way to describe the relationship we've had. As I indicated earlier, I did not meet my father until I was thirteen years old. By the age of thirteen I had encountered many experiences in my life. I had spoken my first words, taken my first steps, lost my first tooth, among many other events. All of these firsts were milestones that he missed. These experiences could never be repeated and obviously, we would not be able to relive the past thirteen years. Some outsiders would say that I should be thankful for the time I've had to spend with my father. In many ways, I absolutely agree with this sentiment. I can say that I am happy that my father cared enough to decide that he wanted to be a part of my life. He really has done his best to establish a relationship with me and I am glad that this has occurred. However, there still lingers some degree of disappointment because there were many things that he missed.

Recently my father's daughter, my half sister, got married. My wife and I attended the wedding and the event was beautiful. On this occasion, I had an opportunity to meet people from my father's side of my family. It was rather awkward because I was 37 years old being introduced as my father's son. I felt somewhat strange because I also met the children of one of my other half-sisters. Strangely enough, her children were actually very close to my age, yet I was their uncle. They told me that they had heard a lot about me and they were excited to meet me. The feeling was mutual; however, we all felt a bit uncomfortable about meeting the way we did.

Attending the wedding also made me realize all that I had missed out on as I was growing up. For instance, my half sister's mother was married to my father; therefore, my half sister grew up with him in her household. She woke up and fell asleep with him there, so he could provide comfort when she needed it. On her wedding day, he was there to walk her down the aisle, giving her away to her future husband. Now, I'm not a female and he would not have given me away, but it got me to thinking about what it would have been like to grow up seeing him every day. So for me and many other *daddiless* children, we can only imagine what it might have been like to share that type of closeness with our fathers. At the wedding, I felt some degree of hurt, as well as, a little jealousy even though I was happy for my half-sister and her new husband.

Being *"on the fringe"* is like being an outsider looking in. You can see everything that is happening, but you are not really part of the action. At times in my life, I certainly felt like I was dressed and ready for the game, but never allowed to play. The old saying *"Close, but no cigar"* comes to mind when I think about the relationship I have with my dad. In the 19th century, it was a practice to give someone a cigar as a prize if they won a game at the carnival. If the person lost the game, the announcer would say *"Close, but not cigar."* In some ways, I felt like I did not win my father's true love. Another saying I heard growing up that really describes the fringe relationship pretty well is the phrase *"close is only good enough in horseshoes and hand grenades"*. So being on the fringe with my father would never measure up to actually winning the prize of having him there as a constant companion and confidant. Anyway, it was not my wedding day so my feelings were somewhat misplaced, but I felt them nonetheless. For me the wedding was a metaphor for a large portion of my developmental years without my father.

I'm sure other children who were *"reunited"* with their fathers have felt a feeling of not being number one in his life. We have felt like something and someone else has, and always will, come before us. This drama could also be played out with a child who's a product of divorce. Daddy has moved out and moved on, remarried, and now has a whole other family, maybe even a new baby. If there are stepchildren, they may or may not like their new father because he is not their *"daddy"*. To compound the issue, there may be a new baby who gets the privilege of growing up and living with *"your father"* while you grow up with your mother (and maybe a stepfather). I'm sure feelings of disappointment and jealousy come into play in these circumstances as well.

I'm positive my father is proud of my accomplishments and of me. I know that he made efforts to bond with my family and me, but despite all of his efforts, I continue to feel like a spectator instead of a participant. I realize the current state of our relationship is partly a result of my own stubbornness, insecurity and inability to trust.

I remember being stubborn when my father and I would not speak to one another for months. It was not because we were fighting or even angry at each other. I had decided that I should not have to call him. I would become upset with my mother when she asked me had I spoken with my father. I would respond by saying *"if he wanted to talk to me then he needed to make the call."* I had taken on the posture that I should not have to be the one to make the first move by calling him; if he wanted to speak with me, he knew my number. I rationalized this by thinking I was the one who initiated our first contact so he should call me if he wanted to continue building our relationship. I decided that he would have to take the necessary steps if he was interested in being in my life. I did not want to feel like I was forcing myself into his life or want him to feel obligated to me, despite the fact that I believed he owed me something. He owed me those calls and when he did not call me and instead I called him, I would feel rejected all over again but I never let him know it.

My father and I still don't talk on the telephone very much, but I did get over the anxiety of calling him; I stopped letting my pride get in the way. I had to find a greater joy by allowing myself to be released from anger and stubbornness so that my children will have an opportunity to experience my father in a way that I did not. I also recognize that it is extremely difficult to establish a true trust relationship with a father who was absent from my life for the first thirteen years. In fact, a lot of us have trouble trusting anyone fully and our fathers are no exceptions.

I know there must be others who have experienced similar fringe situations. What comes to mind are the children of a father who has been incarcerated for years and is now free. I hope they have learned to move courageously past their father's shortcomings. Unfortunately the missing years cannot be recaptured. But you now have an opportunity to make new memories together. It may difficult to embrace the idea but it may be worth a try.

Although he has never given my children birthday presents; nor Christmas presents; and although we infrequently interact during the holidays, I'm glad they at least know who he is and that they have interacted with him. My children's experiences with their grandfather are somewhat closer to the goal and not *"on the fringe"*. Today, I'm ok with that because I have an opportunity to do better by my children and that's a hole in one.

Chapter XX.

MISSED OPPORTUNITIES

Alright, so I decided to write this chapter anyway. I think it's important to discuss the things that are missed by an absent father. Have you ever had a friend or family member who always has a wonderful story to tell? It seems like their experiences are always interesting and exciting. Many of their stories really make you wish you had been there in person to encounter the event firsthand. It is like the party that all the celebrities attended or the event of the year and you missed it. You missed it! Your friends or family members came back telling you about all the free drinks they drank; there were not any fights and to quote another gangsta rapper from his *1993* hit song, it was a *"Good Day."*

In my opinion, any day that you can spend with your child can be a *"good day"*. In a way, I'm trying to convey to all those fathers who have left their children that your life will be enriched when you are actively involved in your child's life. For any father who knows their child exists, the feeling of having missed out on something, especially when it comes to the child, will always be there. But let's explore what he is missing. This person will never see his child's first steps and he will never have an opportunity to hear his child speak her first words. He will not have an opportunity to teach him how to play catch, swim, and ride a bike or shave, for example. It will always be as if he (the father) was *"a day late and a dollar short"*.

Considering these things, the statement *"missed opportunities"* is relative because it is in the eye of the beholder with respect to how they look at the situation. There are some heartless people in this world. Some may believe that it is best that they are not in their child's life; and in some cases, nothing could be truer. Nevertheless, for those mentally healthy, stable, capable individuals who are aware of their child's existence, these are opportunities whether they are viewed that way or not. Despite the fact that a father may not ever want anything to do with his child, I believe these opportunities are not negated just because he chooses not to be in the child's life. Not all of these situations are alike because there are other reasons he may not be involved. In some instances, the mother may be unstable, or the child does not want anything to do with him; the mother has moved the child out of the state or the country, these are some of the things that may impact on these opportunities. But I am mainly talking about those who are choosing to stay away.

Regret for these missed opportunities can vary. It is a shame to think that a child's accomplishments can determine the level of regret that a father may have for these missed chances. Things like seeing their child play little league baseball, witnessing an acting debut, or graduating from high school are just some of the activities that parents are usually grateful for not missing. Imagine that the young person graduated from college, becoming a world-renowned doctor, lawyer or businessperson. What about those children who grew up to become famous actors, athletes or entertainers, will their absent fathers attempt to reappear in their lives to take the credit as well as reap the rewards of other people's efforts?

For example, take a child who becomes a famous basketball player earning millions of dollars. The absent father may take credit for the child being so tall or for the amazing jump shot that was cultivated. What about the famous singer, or dancer, who has an absentee parent step in and unjustly proclaim they are responsible for their singing voice or their great sense of balance? There are times when the father will claim that their genes were the ones that made the child great. Their concern was not for the events that they missed or the upbringing of the child. They have surfaced to reap the benefits of someone else's hard work. They were never there to go through the early stages of developing their child's skills. They were not there for all the Saturday afternoon practices or tournaments. They have never known or made any of the sacrifices necessary to help the child become successful.

Nonetheless, they are willing to come out of the woodwork to celebrate all of the good times, but the question is where were they when times were difficult? They were not there for the heartache that the child felt when they lost a hard fought game or for the elation that went along with winning their first. For these fathers all that seems to count are the high times but not the lows.

The child never forgets the absence of cheers, applauds, or accolades from his or her father. What is even more amazing is that despite these missed opportunities, some of these *daddiless* adults will forgive their fathers and allow them to share in their successes. Regardless of all of his shortcomings, the child is dedicated to their own healing, which is demonstrated by forgiving their father. The child's primary reason for choosing to forgive is because he or she wants to know him as well and be released from the burdens of anger and bitterness. As with most cases relating to *daddilessness, forgiveness* is not always extended and there are those that never let go of their anger. I am definitely not advocating that the *daddiless* child, who becomes a wealthy adult, financially support his or her father or even allow him to be a significant part of his or her life. I am advocating forgiveness and healing by moving forward, away from the negative and towards the positive.

Chapter XXI.

FORGIVENESS AND HEALING (THE MOTIVATION)

Anger, discontentment, hatred, and loathing are various words to describe emotions that *daddiless* children are apt to feel regarding their fathers. Even if you are strong enough to turn a negative *motive* into a positive *motivation,* you still may harbor these ill feelings toward him. So what did all that anger and discontentment get you? Better yet, where did it get you? Anger causes stress, which may result in death. So why put yourself through that trauma? The whole concept of forgiveness and healing can be a radical idea for most *daddiless* children.

Bitterness may linger for a long time and I believe it seizes the *daddiless;* this "feeling" may be the strongest emotion one ever experiences. Some *daddiless* children believe that if they let go of this *"feeling"*, they are conceding to being abandoned by their fathers. Holding on to this bitterness is a way of not yielding to the conviction that their fathers wronged them and that this situation is unfixable. More than anything, I believe *"holding on"* to anger, resentment, etc. is a way to *"hold on"* to some remnants of him. Even if the child never knew who their father was, this man continues to be a topic of discussion.

This person has committed the unthinkable, the unforgivable; he has left his child fatherless. For some, forgiveness is earned, similar to respect. I believe that it is easier to forgive someone when there is an established relationship between the parties. When the individuals know one another it is sometimes easier to forgive because there's a connection. This association may provide *"evidence"* to a person and assure him or her that the person being forgiven will not take the forgiveness for granted. Additionally, when there is an existing relationship, one can inquire about the reason(s) behind the action and determine whether the act was within the person's character or not. This relationship also allows there to be an assessment made as to whether the individual is remorseful based on the attitudes they exhibit.

The idea of forgiveness is something that is difficult to conceptualize for the *daddiless* child who has never known his father. When no relationship exists, one has no idea if the parent is remorseful or what other feelings the father may be experiencing. Thus, the child is primarily left to guess what this parent is thinking. Many times the child's assumption of their father's feelings will be based upon the child's own sense of self and altruism and not on anything they actually know about their father. Depending upon the child's upbringing and relationships, forgiving this unknown, unseen person can be a difficult task. Forgiveness is hard because there are many *"bottled up"* feelings that cannot be expressed to the person who is the object of those feelings. It truly does take an exceptional person to forgive the father he or she has never known.

In my situation, it was somewhat easier to forgive my father because I had established a relationship with him. I had an opportunity to get to know the type of person that he is and to observe the efforts he put forth in order to establish a connection with me. Anger and sadness were not as difficult for me to address; however, forgiveness was a challenge. I looked back over all the years that he was not there, but I also took the opportunity to look at the years that lay ahead of us.

Throughout our time together, I have discovered that my father is a decent man. He has made mistakes, just like we all have, but I came to know that I am not one of those errors. As I thought about forgiving him, I recognized that when I was ready to meet him, he was willing to come. I was thirteen years old and my maturity was just beginning. I now realize that it took a great deal of courage for him to accept my invite into my life and for him to be willing to let me be a part of his after so many years. I do not know all of the facts surrounding why he left in the first place and some part of me is not sure that I want to know. However, I am sure that he would have entered my life sooner if I had taken the necessary steps for that to occur. I also had to acknowledge that after so many years had passed he might have believed that I did not want to know him; so out of fear of rejection, he did not initiate finding me.

A father who has abandoned his child may feel a great deal of shame or embarrassment in knowing he left his child. I am proud my father was not a coward. He *"showed up"* and that made it so much easier for me to let go of some of the negative feelings I had toward him. I say *"some"* because there will always be memories of the days without him and the affect that his absence had on my life. There are still some things that I will not call him about, for example advice on raising my children or marital advice. Nothing against him, our relationship simply never reached a level where we disclosed intimate details of our lives with one another. Today, I am okay with how our relationship has developed. Sometimes I think about how nice it would be to feel comfortable confiding in him and having open dialogue about things that are important. We do not have a very close relationship, but I do appreciate the fact that I know him and he knows me.

When I think about forgiveness, I know that I allowed my pride to interfere for many years; I was too proud to let him know that I was hurt by his absence. I also realized that if I had not taken the steps to meet him we might not have ever met.

Initially, I was prideful because I was responsible for us meeting. In the beginning, I also resented him for *"making"* me, as a thirteen-year-old boy, make such an important decision. Nevertheless, as I have grown, I have kicked arrogance to the curb and realize that I am more grateful to have had the opportunity to know my father than to not know him.

I was instrumental in initiating our relationship, but it was his willingness to set aside his embarrassment and pride so that he could establish a relationship with his son. I am grateful for his courage and willingness to try. Some *daddiless* people reading this chapter may feel that I was weak for feeling thankful that he was brave enough to stand up, even though it was years later. Some may feel that I was weak for not continuing to be hateful. Others may feel that I was weak for *"taking what I could get"* so to speak by allowing him to enter my life after so many years. There may even be those that feel I am making excuses for someone for whom excuses should not be made.

By no means am I condoning his actions, but with age comes deeper understanding and wisdom. Over the years, I have learned that harboring anger and hatred can do devastating things to your mind and body. More than that, holding on to negative feelings does not promote the healing of past hurts. Coming to terms with those feelings is freeing to you and your spirit. More importantly, my relationship with GOD has taught me that forgiveness is required in order to be forgiven.

Making a conscious decision to forgive someone for his or her actions does not necessarily mean the other person's actions are forgotten. It is a sign of growth when a person is able to remember what occurred without holding on to any negative emotions that are attached to the memories. Evidence of true evolution comes when an individual is able to release anger and resentment and move towards forgiveness. Sometimes it is good to remember an unpleasant experience; it allows you to put events into perspective as well as gauge how far you have come. These memories are reminders that things were not always great, but the reflections continue to help you excel, work harder, give 100 percent of your effort, and never give up on what you believe.

More than anything, I believe that forgiving my father helped me to become a better person. I have been able to use those potential *motives* as *motivations*. Forgiving has helped me heal psychologically. My willingness to forgive has allowed me to have relationships that are more meaningful with those I love. I know I am not always the easiest person to get along with; forgiving my father has helped me to understand my flaws and recognize my own mistakes. Living angry is not going to yield anything positive. Pushing those *motives* to their maximum and allowing them to dictate your life's journey is one of the fastest ways to self-destruction and possibly the grave. I have learned that the best way to avenge one's hurt is to prove an individual wrong. When someone declares that you can't, show them that you can.

If you have started down one path, it does not mean that you will end up where others said you would. Sometimes you have to make your own way. For some, the path they choose will lead them to destruction, but for others, starting down that wrong path is just the wakeup call they need. In order to turn yourself around and change your destination, it is necessary for you to learn to forgive. First, forgive yourself for allowing those *motives* to push you in the wrong direction if that is the road you chose. Second, forgive your father for leaving you; it is all right to think of it as his loss. Just look at the wonderful person you are and the life he has missed out on sharing with you because he left you. It is also important to understand that if you are not living right (and caused a lot of problems), then it will make it easier for him to make excuses as to why he stayed away. He may be almost *"grateful"* that he was not around and is absent because he feels like he *"dodged a bullet"* by not having to deal with the drama associated with the negative life his child is living. So why not prove him wrong?

When you release the negative feelings you have been harboring in your heart and spirit, healing will begin and your self-esteem will skyrocket. In order to move forward this is the essential element that must take place before you can truly convert your *motives* into *motivations*.

Chapter XXII.

WHAT MOTIVATED ME?

At a young age, I perceived greatness within me. Even without the initial support and encouragement of a father, I knew that I was destined to accomplish great things. How amazing is that? Where did the *motivation* originate? Was it internal, external, or just supernatural? My mother likes to share the story about me being three years old and telling her that I lost my confidence. She asked me if I knew what the word *"confidence"* meant. I responded, *"When you feel good about yourself"*. My mother then gave me a big hug because she was amazed that I knew the definition of the word. She told me that I could *"do anything and that there is no such word as can't."* That was the beginning of my positive journey. I knew I had to be confident.

In many ways, I was motivated by dissatisfaction. Dissatisfied with our living and financial situations, discontent with people I was surrounded by, and my displeasure with the direction of my life, all became parts of my *motivation*. I wanted more out of life, just like many daddiless children do. The writing was on the wall and the examples were there in front of me. If I did not do anything differently, I was destined for the same result.

I needed to begin making changes while I was young; if I didn't change at that time I would have probably made mistakes that I could not correct later. The people and conditions that were around me could have possibly dictated to me how my life was going to unfold. If I had made the decision to hang in the streets or start hustling drugs, like I had seen so many of my peers do, my life could have taken an undesired turn. Looking for fast money and attention I really did not need could have taken me down the wrong path. I know this is true because I have seen friends and family go to prison and even be murdered, because of those same hasty decisions. If I had let peer pressure and impatience rule me or control my decision-making I would not have reached the level of success I desired.

Today more than ever, so many people are making life-altering choices based on a *"right now"* mentality. Many people are making short-term decisions that have long-term, negative effects. Our *"right now generation"* is not willing to wait for or to accept *"delayed gratification"*. For me, *"delayed gratification"* was a big part of my *"motivation"*. GOD gave me strength and courage to remain patient so I did not engage in destructive activities in order to fulfill an immediate impulse for unnecessary things. I wanted the same things that I saw others enjoy, nice vehicles with rims and a booming sound system. I wanted to have nice clothes that were not from Charity

Newsie, but what was I willing to do in order to obtain those things? Was I going to become a drug dealer? Was I going to have to look over my shoulder constantly for a crack fiend that might knock me upside my head for drugs? Was I going to have to look over my shoulder to avoid the police? Would I worry about other drug dealers who wanted my territory or my customers? Was I willing to sacrifice my life or myself for instant gratification? I decided that patience and discipline were going to be my *motivators*, not immediate satisfaction. In order to be truly successful you will have to make sacrifices and persevere for the long haul.

If I did not have opportunities to gain a different outlook from outside of my living conditions, I probably would not have wanted to leave that environment. I think many people who are subject to living in deplorable surroundings have this mentality; they tend to stay in these living conditions because the surroundings are familiar. In some cases, fear of the unknown keeps them immobile. Therefore, unless one gets the opportunity to compare their environment to something better, their dreadful, familiar conditions are all they know. Some people believe there isn't anything better beyond their current circumstances, so why leave? There has to be something inside a person that makes him or her strive for something better. Numerous factors inspire individuals; their desire for money and personal belongings (similar to the possessions seen on MTV Cribs) may encourage them to work hard to get what they want. I simply possessed a strong desire to live a fulfilling and meaningful life.

One of the most important things to consider is the method you choose in order to obtain what you want. I watched so many of my friends learn how to hustle; I too tried the hustle *"game"* when I was younger. No not drug dealing, but something a little different. There was a man, we'll call Morris, who was a real *"hustle man"*, with the ability to sell ice cubes to Eskimos. Morris drove a white old school Lincoln Continental. The car was kind of run down, but at the time he must have *"earned"* a decent amount of money in order to afford a luxury car like that. He was a plump, round, light-skinned black man, who probably could have passed for white. He looked like he was mixed with Italian. I would say he was about 50 years old, but the most distinct feature about Morris was that he always had a fat stogie cigar in his mouth. Morris also kept a trunk full of cheap trinkets such as zodiac plaques, clothes, necklaces, and costume jewelry that would most definitely turn your neck green, but he knew how to hustle and was still able to sell these worthless items. He would use kids to sell his wares. He also taught some of the older boys how to shine shoes and boots. He would pick the kids up and take them with him to various rodeo types of events. That's where the *"real"* money was; I had no idea that shining cowboy boots could be so profitable, but the boys would come home with serious money.

I would see Morris perusing the neighborhood and picking up my friends; some of them returned with pockets full of money. In those days *"serious money"* translated to ten to fifteen dollars for a full day of work with Morris. In retrospect, they may have actually earned seventy-five to one hundred dollars; however, they received *"chump change"* considering they did all the work. As a kid, in the seventies and early eighties, twenty dollars could buy a lot of candy bars, so I decided to *"earn"* my money too.

One day I told my friends to ask Morris if I could go with them. Initially Morris told them that I was too young and I had to wait a year or two. After about a year or so, I told them to ask him again. This time he agreed; my mother concurred as well. I never knew where they would go to sell the jewelry, but on my first day I sure found out. Morris instructed the kids to enter bars and lounges to sell useless jewelry to drunken adults. I did not realize it at the time, but this was extremely dangerous. In retrospect, the situations and the locations we were stepping into were some of the roughest bars in the city. Places like *"Joe's Hole"* or *"the Cannon Bar"* were just some of the names. In some of the establishments; murders; drug deals; prostitution; fights; stabbings; and shootings were all commonplace. A standoff could erupt at any time; it was extremely dangerous for a twelve or thirteen year old kid to be there and outright illegal for a kid my age.

Morris' idea was effective to some degree, who would deny a cute little kid a dollar for a pair of fake gold earrings? It was a good sales tactic; however, not all adults like kids. Most of the people in those places were probably there to escape from their own children. Therefore, running into a young boy inside their *"waterhole"* could mean trouble. It was not unusual to hear, *"what the hell are you doing in here you little bastard?"* We had some narrow escapes from some of those folks. Fortunately, the bar maids and bartenders were usually friendly. In most cases, I had one of my older, more experienced friends with me and he knew when to *"get the hell out of dodge"* when necessary.

The bad part for me was I did not even get a chance to sale the *"good stuff"*, such as earrings. I was left to sell the pitiful zodiac plaques. If you can remember, they were the brown wooden plaques that had two naked people on them in various sexual positions, which were supposed to represent the zodiac sign. Yeah, those were the useless trinkets that I was commissioned to sell. I guess they were hot back in the seventies, but in the eighties when I was selling them it was like selling pet rocks. Nobody ever wanted to buy those things, not even from a cute little kid like me. I would go home most nights without any money and that got old quick. At that point, I learned, to some extent, that the street hustling game was not for me. Even though I gave up selling trinkets, I chose other types of hustles. I would shovel snow in the winter, perform yard work in the summer, and rake leaves in the fall. I even eventually learned to hook up cable in the spring. Some years later, I obtained a legitimate job and worked before I went to college. My hustling days taught me one important thing and that was to be diverse and to not settle for only one stream of income. I also learned that the life of a street hustler was not for me, so I was inspired to do things legitimately.

Too Embarrassed

My dissatisfaction was all around me and I was motivated by the aspects of my situation that I did not like. Getting clothes from charity was just the tip of the iceberg. I remember days when my mother would send me over to our neighbor's house to ask for a few dollars until she received her welfare check. One day in particular resonates in my mind. It was the first of the month and we had been anxiously anticipating the arrival of the mailman. The first was a very important day for my family and me because that was the day the welfare check would arrive. That was also the day that mom could go and pick up her food stamps.

On this particular occasion, our whole family had been waiting all day for the mailman, *"this messenger of good fortune."* We were hungry because we did not have any food in the house. Now when I say we did not have any food we literally had only flour, sugar, ketchup, and maybe baking powder. The arrival of the welfare check meant we might have a pizza or some special meal that evening, the first of the month was an exciting day for us kids. It was the middle of summer and on this day I actually woke up early. Summers were somewhat harder for mothers on welfare because that meant the kids would be home all day and the money had to be stretched farther because her children were not in school where they would receive breakfast and/or lunch.

We did not have any food for breakfast so I had to wait until the afternoon when the mailman arrived before I could eat. As a 7-year-old boy, I felt as if I was starving to death by the time twelve noon rolled around, but the mailman still had not come. One o'clock came and went, no mailman. One fifteen, no mailman. One thirty, no mailman. So my middle brother and I ran over a few rows of apartments to see if the mailman was on the other block. We did not see him. I asked one of my friends who lived in that row of apartments whether his mother had received her check and he replied that she had not. At this point I'm almost in a full fledge panic. We thought he was never going to come. Back in those days, it was not unusual for someone to break into the mail truck and steal the checks, so there was no telling what might have happened to that man.

At this point, we are even hungrier because we had just exerted our dwindling energy by going out in the hot July sun running about three or four blocks looking for this guy. My brothers and I felt like we were going to die from starvation since we had not eaten all day. We kept asking our mother where he was and she would respond, "*He will be here*". Therefore, at about two o'clock that afternoon lo and behold here comes the mailman strolling down the street. You could have pushed me over with a feather, I was so happy. I mean we were elated to see this *"messenger of joy"*, this *"bearer of bliss."* My middle brother and I both ran up to him and escorted him all the way up to our door. He already had our mail in his hand. As I looked at what he handed my mother the excitement and happiness of the moment was drained from my body and was replaced with horror. In the small stack of mail, I could clearly see that the yellowish- brown envelope the checks came in was missing from the rest of the mail. My mother asked the mail carrier if there was anything else for her. He politely said *"No."* My mother told us to come into the house and she closed the door.

By now I am thinking to myself, oh my GOD what are we going to do? We do not have any money or any food, plus we have not eaten all day. I heard this voice yell out in my head, *"We are going to die."* How are we going to survive? My mother told my oldest brother to go over to Ms. Adams, our neighbor's house and ask her to borrow twenty dollars. He was instructed to tell her that our family's check had not come and she would be paid back when my mother received the check. I am not certain about what type of relationship my mother had with Ms. Adams but I never knew them to talk much with one another. However, on this day Ms. Adams was like my best friend. Fortunately, she loaned my mother the money. My mom then dispatched my eldest brother to the store to buy some bologna, cheese, chips and a two-liter of soda pop. When he came back with the food my mother closed up all the doors, windows and curtains and we had a feast. That was the best bologna and cheese sandwich that I ever had.

I learned a great lesson that day about saving money. I also learned the importance of doing right by people. The other significant lesson I learned from this experience was that I never wanted to live hand to mouth again. There were hard times since that day but not having food to eat was a serious *motivation* for me. Although I discovered there are times when one has to push past pride and potential embarrassment to have their needs met; I never wanted to be that poor again. Embarrassment can be a great *"motivator"*. I did not view these situations as positive when they were happening to me, but in hindsight, I realize that the lessons I learned were extremely beneficial. I am not suggesting that people go out seeking ways to be humiliated; but to have an awareness that if you find yourself in a compromising position it can more than likely work for your good.

Roaches

There were other embarrassing situations I encountered that were *"motivating"* as well. Being a teenager is an important stage in a young man's life that is inherently awkward, but is more complicated when trying to impress girls. As a teenager, having a girl come over to your home was a very big deal. I was always too embarrassed to let a girl know where I lived because our residences were so bad. The outside of our homes looked O.K., sometimes, but when you came into the house, the roaches were so widespread and disgusting that we hated to turn off the lights at night because they would literally be all over the place. Their droppings and eggs would be everywhere. No matter how much we would *"bomb"*, spray, and clean they would always return. The bombs would go off making the pests evacuate like a city at war. Those critters were like something out of a horror movie. We would spray or step on them and it was as if they would look up at us and say, *"Is that all you've got? My little sister hits harder than that!* Then they would turn up a glass of *"Raid"* (not literally), pull out a lawn chair and chill out.

Despite their resilience, one night I decided to have a girl I was dating come over to my house to *"watch a movie."* When she arrived at my place it was just beginning to get dark. As I had hoped, we sat with the lights off and started *"making out"*. This was cool, but as it got darker, my little friends, the roaches, decided they were going to check out the situation. So as we were embarking on a deep and passionate kiss, the only light in the apartment was the television. All of a sudden, the lighting in the room began to change. I looked over at the television and saw a big pregnant roach crawling across the television screen. I was trying to ignore the roach by pulling my date closer and kissing her even more. After a minute or so, the bug decided to move on. Now I know my date saw this huge menace and all the other roaches when I turned on the light to see her out. But she either really liked me or she was so embarrassed for me that she never mentioned our house pests. We kept dating so I guess she really liked me. But this embarrassing situation was another point of *motivation.* This experience taught me that if I worked harder I would not ever have to live in that type of a roach infested environment again.

Toilet Paper

While toilet paper is a staple for most households, the issue of being *"paperless"* seemed to happen more often than not at our house. At times I would get down to the last few sheets on the roll finding myself folding and folding the paper until I could not fold it anymore. When I ran out of paper, I would literally have a mess on my hands. Can you imagine anything worse than sitting on the commode and discovering you do not have toilet paper in your house? Many of us have experienced the dilemma of being stranded on the toilet bowl. Imagine the embarrassment of this situation if you have a guest over and while they are using the restroom someone realizes there is no toilet paper in the house. When we did not have toilet paper in the house my mother would tell my brothers and me, *"You better go in there and get some newspaper and crumple it up and use it"*. Our only other option was to get a washcloth and use it to wipe.

How do you ask your friends or family who's visiting to use a rag to wipe their behinds? How embarrassing is that? How do you tell them that you cannot afford a ninety-nine cent roll of toilet paper because your mother used her last little bit of change to buy a pack of cigarettes? At the time, my mother's *"must haves"* were cigarettes and alcohol so if we ran out of toilet paper after she brought those items we were just out of luck.

These were some of the embarrassing moments that I remember. It may be hard to imagine that something as simple as toilet paper could be a *motivation* for someone. Just go without it for any period of time and you will understand how this can be a serious *motivator*. The struggles and embarrassing circumstances that I faced growing up were truly *motivations* for me. "*That which does not kill you can only make you stronger* ", I learned this lesson the hard way.

Winters Cold

Money or the lack thereof taught me many lessons. My mother taught me how to budget money. During my childhood in the ghetto, I learned many lessons from things that were done wrong, not from things that were done correctly. For instance, spending cash for things like pizza was not a good idea when the cash was supposed to be used to pay our bills, for example the electric, gas, or telephone.

At the time, I could not understand how our utilities would be disconnected when our rent cost almost nothing.

Since we lived in subsidized housing the rent could not have been more than $40 dollars per month. But ever so often, the gas or electric would be turned off. I realized later that the welfare check was not a lot of money in the first place. When my mother would spend her cash on cigarettes, beer, wine, liquor or an occasional pizza at the beginning of the month, the money would dwindle quickly. Many times, before the end of the month, my mother's food stamps and cash were both all gone.

When we moved out of the housing project we moved into houses where the landlord would accept Section 8 payments. Section 8 is a form of government-assisted living. One can move into a house or an apartment in which the government pays a significant portion of the rent and the tenant is responsible for the rest. Typically, Section 8 rent was more expensive if you did not live in the housing project, but if you received Section 8 and chose to live outside the housing projects the renter had more flexibility to decide which neighborhood they wanted to live in. In some cases, a decent house could be acquired. The rent for our house was more expensive so there was less money than we would normally have during a given month. The other thing about living in a house, as opposed to a project apartment, was the cost to heat the place was many times higher.

In the projects, there were vents and radiators all over the place, but we could never properly regulate the heat. Most of the time it was hotter than it needed to be and I would frequently get nosebleeds because the heat was so dry. Anyway, when we moved into the house there was a big difference in the heating costs. The furnace in this particular house, like in many Section 8 houses, did not work very well because it was old. Additionally, the house had drafty windows, which made keeping it warm even more difficult. Since we had become accustomed to being warm, probably warmer than we needed to be, my mother would crank up the heat in hopes of keeping the place warm. Unfortunately, this did not work and it resulted in the heating bills going through the roof.

The gas company offered a program called "*the budget*". This so-called "b*udget*" allowed a customer, my mother, to pay a certain amount of money every month throughout the year, regardless of the actual amount owed. The idea was to allow the customer to keep the gas on when they needed it most mainly during the winter season, even if the gas bill was higher than the customer could afford monthly. Thus, when the customer only paid a certain amount per month, any deficiencies were to be paid during the months when the bills would be less, such as during the spring and summer seasons. The belief was that the customer would be able to catch up on their gas bill during those months. In most cases, just like ours, the bill would become so excessive that the customer would have an arrearage that left them in debt to the gas company, sometimes for many years.

Therefore, if the customer could not reduce the bill during those months when the heating costs were reduced, a bigger problem was created. At some point, their gas was disconnected, leaving a significant amount to be paid. In order for the customer to reestablish their gas service they would be required to pay the whole arrearage in full. When the balance could not be paid they did not get their service restored; it was as simple as that. Unfortunately, this is what happened to us in the middle of winter one year. My mother did not have enough money to pay the gas bill because our rent had increased. Since she had this extreme arrearage, the gas company would not reestablish our gas services. It was extremely cold outside since we were at the peak of the winter season. For an 11-year-old boy there is nothing like walking home from school, in the middle of a bitter cold winter, just to find there is no refuge at home.

The frigid winter was a major *motivation* for me because we were struggling unlike we had ever struggled before. In this particular case, not only did we not have gas, we did not have any food either. My mother only had a few dollars that she used to buy kerosene for the heater my grandfather had loaned us. My grandmother gave us some food and the few dollars she could spare so we could purchase the kerosene. Sadly, the money and kerosene lasted a few days. The weekend had come and the food pantry was not open; besides, there was so much snow on the ground that it would have prevented us from traveling to the pantry even if we did have a car. We were on our own.

Imagine the scene. We are in a freezing cold house, basically in one room and sleeping under multiple blankets. The only heat in the whole house was a single kerosene heater that had to remain on the lowest setting in order to conserve the oil. There is no food in the house and all cooking had to be done on a hot plate or our electric skillet. This was not the best scenario, but here we were. What was strange to me, when remembering these conditions, is that it was very uncomfortable, but at the same time, rather cozy. It was a circumstance that brought our family closer together and that's why I can appreciate the experience. Despite the way I view it today, this was a very rough time because we weren't just cold, we were also hungry.

Since there was not any food or any money, I figured out a plan to get something to eat. It was cold outside and it had just snowed about 6 to 8 inches. We did have a shovel so the most logical way to earn money for food was to shovel snow. I did not have snow boots or gloves so I wore gym shoes on my feet and tube socks on my hands. I remember so vividly every *"no"* that I heard. However, there was one woman who said *"yes."* I was cold and hungry, but I worked my little behind off for five dollars. When she paid me, my hands were freezing and I thought my toes were going to fall off, but I had the money. All that was left for me to do was go to the store and get something for our family to eat. There was a store on the corner. I went in and bought a five-pound bag of potatoes, a pack of margarine, and a 99 cents package of 100 cookies. The cookies were my reward for all my hard work. I dragged my bag, shovel, and five-pound sack of potatoes home, which was a job in and of itself, but I made it. Once I got home, my mother peeled the potatoes and heated up the margarine on the electric skillet so we could enjoy our feast of potatoes and cookies.

This experience was a *motivation* for me because I learned to be resourceful. I had to help my family fill a void; I provided the help they needed. Without my father there to help support our family, I had to become a young man and do what needed to be done. That was the first time I had ever truly contributed to my family's well being and it felt good.

Besides all that, this situation taught me that I should budget my money and have a *"rainy day"* fund. I also learned that getting things via credit was O.K., but paying for them in cash was even better. I never wanted to be obligated to anyone the way my mother was to the gas company. I do my best to pay for everything in cash, except for major items. Today, I do not have any credit cards and I maintain a *"rainy day"* fund. I was truly *motivated* by this situation. I strive to never allow my situation to dictate the direction of my life. All of the situations I have described were truly humbling and they taught me how important it was to have the support of family. I know for a fact that these situations made me more resilient. More than anything, I have learned not to shun the struggle for it is GOD's gift. The struggles taught me to rely on GOD for my help and these situations brought me closer to him.

Family

Family can provide some of the best and worst examples of how you can turn a *motive* into *motivation* or a *motivation* into a *motive*. Relatives can show you the benefits of breaking generational curses, how to express love and what it feels like to receive love. Family can also help you to establish values that help to mold your life. Family members can reveal to you some of the underlying secrets that may have been crippling or holding your family back for many generations.

Conversely, family can also provide you with examples of behaviors that you should avoid. A family can help by supporting you in your situations or it can possibly make the situations worse. Fortunately, I had a really good foundation. Even though I did not have my father, I did have my family. I have always had a mother who loves me, probably more than she loves herself. Without her love I know my life would not have been the same. We may not have had much but we have always had love. I also had aunts and uncles who cared about me enough to show me alternatives to my circumstances. They gave me opportunities to experience life outside of the struggles and hardships I witnessed in the ghetto. My grandmother and grandfather demonstrated (for me) a positive example of marriage. They fed me, molded me, and helped shape me into a positive young man, despite all of the negative things I had experienced.

My aunts and uncles would take me to their homes on weekends to give me a reprieve from our sometimes tumultuous living arrangements. They allowed me to earn money, legally, without having to hustle. I would beg them to pick me up or I would walk miles to get to their houses in an effort to escape. In some ways I was ensuring that I had a good meal, but it also provided me with a means of leaving the hard-core life that went along with growing up in the rough neighborhoods where we lived.

Many of the people that were around me influenced my way of doing things, my desires, my mind, and my goals. I still run into many of my childhood friends; it is sometimes sad to see how their lives have unfolded. Many, if not most, of them were in the same or similar situations as my family and unfortunately, they currently remain in these unpleasant circumstances. Still perpetuating the curses that were cast upon them by their parents, they live the same way that their parents did.

Lots of the females I grew up with later had multiple children who are now *daddiless*. Some of the women are not formally educated, despite the fact that they were extremely smart. Although they were highly intelligent, they lacked a clear plan for their lives; they were only familiar with the block they lived on and the people who lived there. For those who were still living in undesirable environments, they did not know how to change their mindsets in order to achieve a better life. Many did not know how to improve their situations and continued to live in their deplorable, yet familiar, environments. Like so many others from my neighborhood, these individuals carried on the generational curses they had experienced. Some of them did not have the same family support system I did. In fact, it may have been the examples displayed by their family members that prevented them from improving their lives. If they wanted more out of life they did not have much help. I believe underprivileged people like me are stronger, or at least more resourceful, than most people because they sometimes improve their lives without much assistance from others, including their families. I commend them for their courage and fortitude in making their lives better.

Some men were unsuccessful at leaving these negative environments and became street hustlers who fathered multiple children out of wedlock. Many of the children do not know their fathers and the fathers don't know their children. Some have children that they know, but with whom they have very little interaction; they acknowledge their children, but do not make it a priority to see or invest in them. They live day-to-day trying to get by, while denying the pain that *daddilessness* has caused their children. These are the guys that come out of the woodwork if their children become famous or wealthy; they come around when things are good and hope to reap the rewards of their child's hard work. They will try to take credit for giving their children the *"good genes"* that made them the people they have become. They often express how *"proud they are of them"* for all of their accomplishments and reminisce about that one visit they shared so many years ago. In most cases, the compliments and ego stroking means very little, but the child is so excited about having their father in their life so he or she overlooks their negative history. This is forgiveness at the highest level.

Family is an ideal source to help you determine what you want out of life and the people you want in your life. You should take note of and try to follow the positive examples you see within your family. I hope that your observations will help you to decide how you desire your life to develop. My relatives were the best example because I knew they loved me and were willing to work to keep me in line, as well as out of trouble. Hopefully, there are family members that fit the bill in your life who can serve as the examples you need to be better.

Alcoholism and Drugs

The issues of alcoholism and drugs have really been a big *motivation* in my life. In some ways, I wonder if my father had been present would my situation have been the same. Would I have been sheltered from the kind of life we lived or the environment if he was present? Would my mother have been so addicted to alcohol? Maybe this is just wishful thinking on my part, but I would like to believe that had my mother been in a stable relationship with my father it would have made my life so much better.

There were positive things that my father could have brought to the table, like having a stable job. He is a skilled carpenter, which translates to more financial stability. My father is an extremely hard worker. Despite the fact he has retired twice, he still continues to perform remodeling jobs and serves as the disc jockey for his lodge. This kind of a work ethic and resourcefulness would have served as a shining example for any child to observe every day; too bad I did not have that opportunity.

More than anything, I believe that if my father was there my mother would not have been subjected to the domestic abuse that she went through for so many years. In many cases, domestic violence goes hand in hand with alcoholism and drug abuse. In my mother's case, I believe that her alcoholism was one of the main reasons that she stayed with her abusive boyfriend for so long. I recall an instance when my mother was beaten so badly by her drug addict boyfriend that she was admitted to the hospital with a massive concussion. The trauma was so intense that when she returned home she began to hallucinate and have flashbacks of the tragic ordeal that had occurred there.

Alcoholism and drugs had negative physical and psychological implications for our family, but it resulted in severe financial consequences as well. I watched how much money was spent, more like wasted, on the consumption of alcohol. In many instances, our house was the local watering hole. At one point there was more money spent on alcohol than on food, or anything else for that matter. During one summer, things were so bad we did not have any gas or electric in the house, but every day the *"watering hole"* was full with beer, wine, and liquor. It was obvious where their priorities were. Watching these individuals waste their money and their lives on frivolousness really gave me the opportunity to witness first-hand the things I did not want to do with my money or my life. It also provided me with a chance to see the long-term effects that alcoholism could have on a person.

Many of the people that would hang out at our house were some of the local drunks. I had some of the best examples of what not to do with my life. Most of these people, including my mother, would spend almost all of their days sitting out in a dirt lot in the back of the house getting drunk. Lots of these drunks had no further ambition for their lives but to drink all day every day. I saw what it was like for a person to truly get *"pissy drunk"* and make a fool of himself or herself.

Unfortunately, I was not the only one who observed this happening; my middle brother did too. Despite all of the negative aspects of this negative behavior, my middle brother chose this same route for his life. He even took it a step further and became a drug addict; he subsequently went to prison twice. It is no wonder that my brother took this path. So many children who grow up seeing alcohol and drug abuse follow their parent's example because this is what constitutes normal behavior for them. Is there a correlation between being *daddiless* and being an alcoholic or a drug addict? *Daddilessness* creates feelings of depression, hopelessness, emptiness, hurt, anger, and frustration. Many of these feelings lead to harmful behavior such as excessive drinking and illegal drug use; so it is very reasonable to conclude that *daddilessness* can play a heavy role in alcoholism and drug abuse. A *daddiless* child will attempt to fill a void, a proverbial hole in their soul by using alcohol and drugs to medicate the pain. If they do not know how to fill these voids in a healthy manner, it can easily lead to destruction for either the *daddiless* child or someone else, possibly at the hands of the child. I know now that alcohol addiction runs in my family. I also know that it was by the grace of GOD that I never allowed alcohol to control my life. Actually, I have never liked the taste of beer, wine, or liquor so it has never been a problem for me. Thank you Jesus!

During my college years, I indulged in casual drinking and even drank a few times until I was actually drunk. Despite these isolated incidents, alcohol has not been a vice of mine. However, I know that I can be just one drink away from becoming an alcoholic. Armed with this knowledge, I decided about 11 or 12 years ago that I would abstain from drinking alcohol. I will not even take an occasional drink because I don't think it is worth the risk. Knowledge is power and since I knew that casual drinking could lead to alcohol abuse, at least in my family, I figured it was best not to play with fire at all. This may seem extreme to some people, but I have learned that if you know your potential weakness, it's best that you don't tempt fate. If more people recognized this truism then they might find it easier to avoid self-destructive behaviors, which allows them to transform the *"motive"* into a *"motivation"*.

Drugs and alcohol have taken away too many fathers from their children. Most children of drug addicts and alcoholics would prefer not to have anything to do with their parents, especially when they are in the grips of their addictions. When and if, the father is able to begin recovery for his addiction the child may still not want anything to do with him. In many cases, the father has made some very serious decisions that would indicate that he is more concerned with his drugs or alcohol than he is with his own child. We are talking about decisions that have led the child to either feeling abandoned or actually being abandoned. How does a child get over being substituted for a drug? We all have heard the horror stories about drug-addicted parents selling their babies for crack and babies being born addicted to drugs. The ramifications and feelings associated with this epidemic of drug and alcohol addiction can absolutely translate to *motives or motivations*. It is really up to the child to decide which direction he or she will go.

In many cases, it is the *daddiless*ness that helps to instigate the drug situation; many times both instances go hand in hand. A child who is abandoned or left to be raised by his or her mother, another family member, or the foster care system, may turn to drugs or alcohol in order to *"fill"* their emptiness. Clearly, this is not the most appropriate method to handle this situation, but again, the *motive* can begin with daddy not being there.

A strong sense of family can be a great way to address this *motive*. I had a sense of belonging, a great sense of love from my mother and my other relatives, I was able to avoid the pitfalls that drugs and alcohol can bring. There is no way I can take the credit for not becoming a drug addict. I actually experimented with drugs and alcohol early in my life. It was by the grace of GOD that I was able to stay away from that life.

My middle brother was not so fortunate. He saw the lifestyle and the things that went along with getting high and he seemed to like it, at least for a while. Back in the day, my middle brother was *"the man."* When he was in middle school and the early parts of high school, I admired him greatly. My brother had some of the nicest looking girls in our neighborhood and even some from other areas. The girls would come to our run down apartments and pick him up in their nice little cars. He would have decent clothes, usually borrowed from his friends, who were some of the *"coolest"* kids in the neighborhood and at his school. People also admired how well he could handle himself physically. My brother could really fistfight. To this day, some of the guys who grew up with him tell me stories about the epic battles that he had with guys at school or in the neighborhood. I think people would underestimate his fighting skills because he was a *"light-skinned pretty boy."* So here's a guy with pretty girls, nice clothes, and he could fight; he was a triple threat.

Early on, his drug and alcohol use consisted of smoking marijuana and drinking 40 oz bottles of beer. After a while, things began to change and some of the fine girls became pregnant. Now, it was not just all fun and games; he was now a father a few times over. The fighting began to take a toll on his looks and his drug and alcohol abuse increased dramatically.

Eventually, he got kicked out of high school because he would ditch class frequently. Even when he did go to school he would get into fights or he would attend class while drunk or high.

I can recall my mother being called to the school during one of his episodes because he was observed by the school staff drinking a 40oz bottle of beer while walking down the school hallway. Ultimately, my brother did graduate, but it was not from high school. He graduated to drinking hard liquor and using even harder drugs. This subsequently resulted in his crack addiction and then criminal behavior to feed the addiction. This behavior eventually resulted in his imprisonment. My brother's choices led him to a continuation of the cycle of *daddilessness* that he had experienced. I'm sure that he regrets some of the choices that he made so early-on; but most of all, he regrets not being there for his children while they were growing up. It is truly unfortunate that some of his children may feel many of the same negative things towards him that he may have felt towards his father. I'm not sure if the *daddilessness* was the main *motive* for my brother, but I know it played a role along the way.

It's amazing that we all were raised by the same mother in the same household, because we all made different choices. My choices were more like my eldest brother's in that we both went to college. My eldest brother takes care of his responsibilities, but we both wonder what happened with our middle brother. Currently he is out of prison, but still struggles daily with his addiction. I know he is doing his best, most of the time, to make his situation better. The challenge is that the street life is a big part of him and he has difficulty letting it go. I am proud to say that at the time I wrote this book he is working a job and living sober.

His four children have taken different paths in their lives as well, despite the fact that he was not always around. Some have continued the cycle of *daddilessness*, some have gone to college, while others have been in legal trouble. Overall, I am proud of them all and they are doing well, given their circumstances. They are working to create productive lives and I know all of them strive to use their *daddilessness* as a *motivation* instead of a *motive*. My brother's life was really one of the best examples of how choices can affect the lives of others. More than anything, I love my brother for who he is and not for what he has done.

The lessons I learned from my years of watching people drink and drug their lives away was that it can happen to anyone. Seeing others destroy their lives with the use of alcohol and drugs has taught me to work hard at not repeating the patterns of abuse that I saw. Trying your best to avoid those things that can drain your will to survive is very important. Drugs and alcohol can side track and even kill some of the most talented, beautiful, and intelligent people. It really does take courage to just say no when everyone else is saying yes. Work hard to rise above your circumstances so that the *motive* of drug and alcohol abuse can be overcome and it can serve as a *motivation*.

Chapter XXIII.

EASILY INFLUENCED

Webster's dictionary defines the word *"influence"* as *"power exerted over the minds or behavior of others; to have an effect on the condition or development of."* In some situations, it is easy to see the effect that not having a daddy can have on a child. In many cases where daddy is gone, the child may be easily influenced. Without those guiding words of wisdom that a father can sometimes give, it becomes easier for a child to be pulled in by the words of another. When there are different things pulling on a kid, some positive, others negative, the strongest one wins. The amount of influence outside sources have on the *daddiless* child can depend greatly on the environment in which the child grew up.

Fathers are supposed to serve as a sounding board, the voice of reason, the voice of caution, but most of all, the voice of love that assures you everything is going to be okay, even in the roughest times. When daddy is absent, a child may lack clear guidance and not know the difference between right and wrong. When this happens, it makes it possible for almost anyone to come in and exert their influence on the child. Unfortunately, this includes the wrong influences as well. I think about my relationship with my children as they grow; I have noticed them emulating things I have done. They would repeat things I have said, copy my mannerisms, and displayed my habits; it became part of their behavior. Some of my actions at times were positive and others negative. The old saying *"do as I say, not as I do"* resonates very loudly in my mind. I definitely do not want my children to emulate any bad behavior I might exhibit. At the same time, I hope to pass on all of my good characteristics and be a living example of decency and respectability for my children to emulate. It is easy for me to see how my influence can affect my children because they are young and impressionable. Since they are so vulnerable, I must be careful in the things I do and say. I believe my children trust me and know that I would never tell them to do anything that would hurt them.

Additionally, I teach them valuable life lessons; cleaning their rooms, taking care of their possessions, not talking to strangers, trusting GOD etc, are things that they will carry into adulthood. Without that guidance they may not ever know who to trust or what they should and should not do. You must also factor in a stranger's influence on a *daddiless* child. Outside influences can infiltrate a person's life in many ways and as parents we hope what has been instilled in them from an early age will help our kids make excellent decisions and not allow others to take advantage of them.

Are *daddiless* children more apt to be influenced by others due to their desire for acceptance? How badly do you want to fit in? How badly do you want to be a part? Are you willing to do anything for approval? When you've never had a family and experience rejection by your father, this may have a serious affect on how you react when someone shows you attention or tells you that they love you. Not all *daddiless* people are gullible, but are usually skeptical and untrusting towards others; alternatively, they sometimes trust too much. The amount of influence that you allow someone to have over you due to your *daddilessness* can be a *motive* or a *motivation* to trust or not to trust.

You hear it all the time from the kids who join gangs. "*The gang is my family, they took me in and showed me love when no one else would.*" Without that initial foundation that a father can provide, the negative influences can rise up and take over. For example, if a person is already angry about their situation and their environment, it becomes much easier for someone else to come in and make them feel that their way is the better way. If a person is hungry or homeless and someone takes them in and gives them food, the person on the receiving end may be more likely to allow that person to exert influence over him or her much faster than if the situation were different.

Either you're a leader or you're a follower. One of the determining factors as to which one a *daddiless* child will become depends upon the level of self-confidence that the child possesses. The issue of self-confidence is not just isolated to *daddiless* children. However, the circumstances of being *daddiless* play a greater role in the amount of self-confidence a child may cultivate. It's not unusual for many *daddiless* children to suffer from low self-esteem. Daddies play an important role in their children's self-confidence. For example, if no one's present to reiterate to children that they are doing a good job, tell them they are smart, that they made a great play on the field, or say they are proud of their accomplishments, the children may not realize they are on the right path. When children know they are dealing with life properly they become inspired and motivated to continuously work hard and excel. The small acknowledgements and encouragements that are missing can lead a child to believe that he's not doing well or not being responsible. This can occur in a *daddiless* situation or in a situation where a daddy is present but not very attentive.

If a child lacks self-confidence, he or she may follow the wrong people. The encouragement and recognition of a parent is and can be some of the greatest joys a child experiences. Even if a coach or teacher tells a child how well he or she is doing, it is not as impactful as compliments given from mom or dad. Parents are the people who are meant to love their children unconditionally and the children want their approval more than anything. Therefore, a word from mom or dad really has a greater influence on a child than words from anyone else or at least you would hope so. A parent should be the person that a child can trust more than anyone else; when that trust is lost it is difficult to reestablish.

Trust can be lost in a number of ways, a parent not being present at all or making too many broken promises may have this affect. The trust level can either make or break the relationship. Individuals with low self-esteem are sometimes more likely to be taken advantage of because they are too eager to trust; in other cases, some won't trust at all. You hear about the child who decides to follow the crowd. In many of these situations the child has trusted others more than they trusted their parents.

I recall a situation my middle brother was involved in which illustrates this point. In this particular criminal enterprise, my brother decided he was going to hang out with his friend on a street corner. His friend decided to snatch a woman's purse. Obviously, when he snatched the purse both boys began to run. They ran for a short time and were subsequently caught. I believe they were caught by a Good Samaritan who came along to help this defenseless woman, but

I can't recall exactly. Anyway, both boys were arrested and taken to the juvenile detention center. Since this was the first criminal incident that my brother had been involved in, my mother went to court for his hearing. At the time, the magistrate informed my mother that since this was my brother's first offense he would be released to her custody. The other boy was going to be held since he was identified as the person who snatched the purse and his family did not attend the hearing.

At that point, my mother was ready to take my brother home and, lo and behold, he jumps up in front of the magistrate and says, *"If he stays, I stay."* My mother was stunned at this revelation. She responded to the magistrate, *"Keep him!"* Consequently, he stayed in the detention center for two additional weeks and called home every day begging my mother to come and get him. In order to teach him a lesson, she left him there for the two weeks. She would visit him while he was there, but she wanted him to learn. Ironically, the friend that he was desperately trying to stay with was sent to another facility a day or so after court. In the end, all the drama he caused was in vain.

Now, I have no idea what possessed my brother to say something that stupid, but he did; maybe he knew what my mother was going to do to him when he got home. He may have thought staying locked up made him a man. At any rate, this misguided and ignorant decision was the beginning of his criminal career.

I really do not know why my brother was so insecure, maybe it was because he was *daddiless*, but he allowed the influence of his *"so called friend"* and subsequent fellow gang member to supersede my mother's influence. Falling victim to the wrong influences can mean the difference between life and death. Avoiding the influence of the wrong people takes a great deal of courage. Like I said earlier, it takes courage to say *"no"* when everyone else is saying *"yes"*. Courage is required to do your own thing and not be pushed into doing something just because everyone else is doing it. One must be brave enough not to allow peer pressure to influence him or her. You have to be strong and fearless in order to avoid making poor choices just for acceptance. For a child, and even for some adults, I know this is a difficult task, but you cannot allow your fear to dictate your future when making life-changing decisions.

Parents should closely observe the people with whom their children associate. They can proactively influence their children and try to convince them that engaging in negative behaviors for attention, *respect, etc.,* will only lead to jail or something worse. Give your *daddiless* child your attention; keep them involved in positive activities; encourage them to do their best; reassure them and be a *motivation* for them to do good things, not allowing a lack of confidence to be a *motive*.

Chapter XXIV.

"WHAT IF?"

One of the most dominant questions we face growing up *daddiless* is the question of *"what if?"* Throughout this book, I have been asking questions relating to the possibilities of what could have been. For *daddiless* children the question of *"what if"* can plague us for the rest of our lives. If you allow it too, it can become all consuming, devastating your existence. I want to change the perspective about looking at the *"what if"* in your life. I would like you to shift your thinking away from the possibilities of what could happen if your father comes back into your life; this may never happen, so it's pointless to dwell on it. While it is all right to hope, it is not practical to fool yourself and believe he must be involved in your life for you to be happy.

What's amazing about possibilities is that they are endless, as long as you do not limit yourself. The potential in your life can be so great that it is hard to imagine sometimes. My wife always says, *"You have what you say."* So if you say you want something, anything, just add action to your statement and you can have it. You can change you situation by believing it will change and taking the proper steps to ensure the change happens.

Everything in life will not always happen the way you want it to. It may not even happen when you want it to, but it can happen. Sometimes, something different from what you were expecting occurs, but it ends up working out for your good. There are some situations you can control and there are others you cannot. To be successful and to minimize disappointment (in your life), you should focus on things you can influence or affect. You really need to believe that there is power in your *"what if"*. If you believe in yourself enough, not relying on others to determine your destiny (like your father coming back), then you enhance your personal power. You never want to give your power away to someone else. You do not want to allow someone else's persuasion or situation to dominate yours. You must believe in yourself and depend on you. You have to earn your own education, no one can obtain it for you. You must establish your career, no one can work the job for you. Raise your children, no one should have to do it for you.

So your *"what if"* truly does begin with you and no one else. You are *"the captain of your fate, the master of your soul."* Do not ever allow someone to take your power away. You are your own person, made in the image of GOD. No person should be allowed to determine your destiny, your goals, or your *motivation*. I want to encourage all readers of this book to pursue their *"what if"*, viewing it as a new beginning instead of an ending. *"What if"* you became a doctor or a lawyer, *"what if"* you found a cure for cancer or AIDS, *"what if"* you helped others to be *motivated* to accomplish greater things. You may be that person who can bring fathers and their children together, a catalyst for change. So go out and achieve your passion. *"What if"* you do? Why don't you pursue your goals and see what happens?

Chapter XXV.

SO WHAT "MOTIVATES" YOU?

Are you looking to your family and those who love you for guidance and inspiration? Are you looking at the positive role models that you have in front of you or are you watching MTV Cribs, desiring what other people have acquired without wanting to put in the required work to obtain it? Are you using the fact that your father was not in your life as a *motive*, a crutch, or an excuse to be irresponsible? Are you willing to hurt, plot, and scheme to get the things you want? Are you perpetrating the generational curses that have plagued your family for years? Are you allowing division between you and your father to keep you trapped in a negative environment surrounded by destructive people and things?

Alternatively, are you viewing *daddiless* as a *motivation* or a catalyst, propelling you to strive for more? Are you willing to delay your gratification while putting forth the effort to earn what you want in life? Are you more concerned with keeping up with what your friends have and not willing to wait? Things that come later are greater; so be patient. If you work for what you want you will be proud of yourself and you'll reap the rewards of your hard work. Furthermore, you can take pride in knowing that you did not cause harm to others in obtaining your goals. A wise person told me that many things can be taken from you, but knowledge cannot. Once you have learned something it cannot be taken back. A car can be repossessed, an education cannot.

I am a living example that if you set your mind to anything, *daddiless* or not, you can do it. Over the years, I have learned that pain is a temporary inconvenience. Trouble won't last always. Unfortunate situations occur from time to time, but what really matters is how you deal with the pain or frustration. Do not believe that everyone and everything is against you. Times can and will get hard, that is just the normal course of life. Every day is not going to be sunshine and flowers. You are guaranteed to experience some adversity in your life. If you never experience trials or tribulations, you will not appreciate the good times.

Be inspired to do well and when things do not go your way, be ready to try a different method. Sometimes a fresh perspective is just what is needed. Throughout the course of writing this book I have found myself asking questions and expressing feelings that have in some ways acknowledged and/or perpetuated the m*otives* and *motivations* that I have judged or misjudged others as having employed. In some ways, I have found myself relating to things that may make me appear hypocritical or as if I am blaming everything that has happened in my life on being "*daddiless*." I do attribute some of my life issues to being *daddiless*, but my hope is that this expression of my feelings does not come across as if I am making excuses. My true desire is to encourage people not to use being *daddiless* as an excuse for doing wrong.

I believe that the positive and the negative things that I have done in my life have been part of the choices that I have made. These were my decisions, not someone else's. However, I have tried to use being *daddiless* more as a *motivation* versus a *motive*. More than anything, I want you to know that some obstacles you face, because you're *daddiless*, can be overcome; don't allow them to defeat you. Being *daddiless* should not be the overarching theme of your life; do not be a victim! *Motives* can become *motivations* and troubles will soon pass no matter what. You can break the cycle and be the daddy or loving parent you never had.

Chapter XXVI.

DISCIPLINE, SACRIFICE, AND PATIENCE

Demonstrating discipline in a *"right now generation"* is more difficult than can be imagined. In today's society, many things are available instantaneously and it is difficult to be disciplined or patient enough to accomplish goals. People make New Year's resolutions they barely keep past the first quarter of the year; they promise to stop using drugs, smoking cigarettes, drinking alcohol excessively, or they may promise to lose weight. People today are more prone to seek out the quick fix or the short-term *"cure"*, even though they have a long-term issue. We look to patches, pills, gizmos, and gadgets to generate the results we seek. There is no quick fix for the pain and hurt that is caused by being *daddiless*. In order to overcome the *motives* that are created by these situations you will have to be disciplined, make sacrifices, and be patient.

For *daddiless* children, who want to change their *motive* into a *motivation,* discipline is absolutely necessary to accomplish your goals. I remember being in high school and my best friend and I had a weekly one on one game of basketball. After we got out of school and finished our homework we were allowed to go over to the local elementary school to shoot hoops until it was dark. While we were out on the playground, we would occasionally hear the pounding of two 10 or 12 inch woofers speakers in the back of one of our schoolmates tricked out Chevy Cheviot. It had the gold Daytons on it with the low profile tires. This kid was a little older than we were, but he had the booming system and the nice ride. The system was so loud and low that when he came down the street you could hear him from a block or more away. The system would blare to the point that it would rattle the windows of most houses on the street and set off many car alarms. This was in the 1980s when selling crack was at its peak. Most of the kids that we went to school with were hustling drugs and making big money at it.

    My best friend and I admired the things these guys possessed; the freshest clothes, the nicest cars, and the best-looking girls in school. We were both poor; his mother and father were divorced and neither of us had any significant material items. We were there shooting jumpers and missing lay ups, talking about all of the things that we wanted out of life and our plans to achieve them. More than that, we were talking about all of the reasons why we were not going to sell dope in order to get those things. We felt that the risks outweighed the reward. The money was good, but there were other constants that were not so desirable. You'd constantly be looking over your shoulder; constantly looking out for other drug dealers; constantly looking for the police; and crackheads.

That day, while playing basketball, we both decided we would get *"ours"* the legal way by attending college and earning our degrees. I always dreamed of one day becoming a lawyer and he dreamed of becoming an accountant. We avoided doing things illegally so we could avoid *"constantly looking over our shoulders"*. This decision came with a price. We would have to be patient. We would have to avoid the traps that were laid before us. We could not take the microwave approach to life. This life-changing decision meant walking or taking the bus instead of driving ourselves, going hungry sometimes, when other people ate; we worked part-time jobs after school instead of selling crack. We chose to do without until we were able to achieve our goals legitimately.

Our choices created moments of happiness and sadness. I lived without nice clothes or a decent car until I got out of college and could afford one. When I did get my first car, in high school it was a piece of crap and one of the wheels almost fell off. Fortunately, I was resourceful and I learned how to fix the wheel when it broke. When the car leaked oil, I learned how to change a valve cover gasket. When it leaked power steering fluid I learned how to use sealant.

Even when people laughed at my clothes and shoes I remained positive. When I didn't have the finest girls in school chasing after me I still stayed optimistic because I was still doing things legally. So when many of the popular guys who sold drugs were going off to prison, or even being murdered by their rivals, I was still working at Wendy's to put food in my stomach and earn some money in order to get a few of the things I wanted for myself.

Where are they now and where am I now? When I see people from the old neighborhood, I inquire about how some of the popular kids are doing. I discover that a great number of them are either dead, in jail, or on drugs. Others made it through those times of living in the fast lane; however, they do not have anything to show for it today other than maybe a felony conviction or a hard time obtaining work. I used to admire what some of these men or women had when we were growing up, but I knew that lifestyle would provide short-term gains for life-long needs. It was obvious that their financial gains would be short lived. Thank God I was able to obtain an education. My education is immensely valuable. Tangible items, such as cars, money, and clothes, depreciate over time; education appreciates. You can continue to build on your educational foundation once it is established, while a car just gets rusty.

My patience paid off and here you are reading my book. I may not have the best of everything, but I don't have to want for much of anything; this is by the grace of GOD. It took a great deal of time for me to obtain my law degree; four years of college, with no money to pay for it, three years of law school, and a bar passage. All of these years of work have afforded me the opportunities I have been fortunate enough to have. I expended a lot of money and energy. I had to exercise discipline when studying, I sacrificed my time, but mostly, I had to be patient with myself. My best friend and I chose to be mature and do the right thing. I attribute our maturity to being *daddiless* because when daddy isn't present you're forced to grow up quickly. There may be times when you're asked to make adult decisions, but you're still a child.

If you make the conscious decision to be self-disciplined, self-motivated, and self-assured you can achieve whatever your heart desires. As a *daddiless* child, I can relate to and understand that even if you cannot depend on anyone else, you can depend on GOD and yourself. Trust yourself and believe that if you pursue it, you can do it. I'm living proof you can overcome some of the most negative *motive* situations.

Chapter XXVII.

INSPIRATION COMES FROM WITHIN AND FROM DOING WITHOUT

Plato said, *"Necessity is the mother of invention."* Even in this quote there begs the question, where is daddy in all of this? Technically, this quote was not specifically intended to relate to families; however, it can refer to family situations when daddy is absent. In many cases, the necessity is created by the absence of a father so it only makes sense to look to the mother to be the creative innovator and resolve the family's problems. It sounds like even in the time of Plato, *daddilessness* was an issue. Necessity will always translate inspiration to action. The question then becomes are you only allowing external forces to inspire you or do you realize that inspiration comes from within? In many *daddiless* circumstances, there appear to be more challenges that manifest themselves; but not every challenge is the result of one being *daddiless*.

Some situations arose because of decisions made by others even before we were born. We just end up having to suffer the consequences of those decisions. Sometimes it can be the things you want to change that inspire you to do things differently. Whether it's the place where you live or the people you live with, these factors can inspire you to make changes. Positive external influences may not always be present, so it's best to look to GOD and look internally to be inspired. If your encouragement comes from within there is a desire that builds inside of you that makes you want to do better and be better. When you are inspired from within it will not be necessary to have encouragement or approval from others in order to strive for improvement. It has been said that the *"the biggest room in the world is room for improvement."* I think this means you can always improve something about yourself. No external force in this world can *motivate* you in the same way that you can motivate yourself. If you rely on your internal *motivation*, your internal drive, and your internal attitude, no one can ever take that away from you. So even when you have gotten over the anger of being *daddiless,* even when you have escaped the ghetto, even when you have left that abusive situation, you can depend on yourself to keep you going and wanting the best.

Always strive to be the best you can be; do this for yourself and not just to prove something to your father because he was absent. Do this because you love you. Doing *"without"* sometimes makes us stronger while also building character. For example, when you are hungry, you learn how to hunt or you will starve. If you need shelter, you learn to build or you will die from the elements. If you are left behind, you must learn how to move on or you will be stranded in the same place forever. So there is strength in surviving difficult situations. In the thoughts of Plato, when something needs to be accomplished individuals will usually find a way to do it.

More than anything else, I want *daddiless* children to understand that they should not allow themselves to be stuck in a trap by waiting for some external force to motivate them to move. I encourage them to be moved by their passions, not by a desire to attain tangible possessions. No one can change you but you have the ability to change yourself.

Chapter XXVIII.

MY FATHER CHANGED MY LIFE

In this final chapter, I want to recognize how my father has truly changed my life. The title of this chapter may be somewhat misleading because I may not be referring to who some readers might think I am. As I said before *"anybody can be a father, but not everybody can be a daddy"*; however, the father that I am speaking about is a daddy to the *daddiless*, a mother to the motherless, a teacher in the classroom, a lawyer in the courtroom, a doctor in the operating room; he is the true life-changer. Not taking anything away from or adding anything to the contribution my earthly father made in my life, but nothing he has done will ever compare to the way GOD has changed my situation.

Throughout this book, I have expressed my feelings about being *daddiless*. I have also explained how I learned to forgive my (earthly) father. The ironic thing is that I learned forgiveness from my (spiritual) father. It was the word of GOD, my heavenly father's words, that changed my heart and changed my life. In my mind, there was nothing my earthly father could do that would lead me to forgive him, but as I got to know him and as I became stronger in my faith, forgiveness became much easier. In the bible, Matthew 6:14 says, *"For if ye forgive men their trespasses, your heavenly Father will forgive you."* I truly needed to repent to GOD for all of the negative feelings I had for this man. I needed and wanted GOD to forgive me for how I felt about him. My earthly father is a good man and he made an error in judgment in deciding to walk away from me. I had to recognize that and ask GOD to change my heart. Maybe you are in the same place that I was concerning your father. Maybe you don't feel like you can ever forgive him. I am here to tell you that you can if you want to. As I said before, there is healing and deliverance in forgiving. All you have to do is trust and know that even if your father made the biggest mistake of his life by leaving you, you were never alone.

GOD has never abandoned you and you will never have to face life alone. You must believe that GOD, your heavenly daddy, is always present and that he will never leave you nor forsake you; this will make it easier to forgive your earthly father.

Being *daddiless* is an epidemic in America, as well as around the world. It is my desire that this book will help people begin the process of healing and realizing that being *daddiless* is not the end of the world. Use that negative situation as a *motivation* to be greater, to do great things in your life. It is my hope that this book will help to break generational curses, to build stronger families, and help all children contribute positivity to society. I also want this book to create dialogue throughout this world in hopes of breaking the bondage that *daddilessness* produces. I want fathers who are in their homes to begin to talk to their children, learn their interests, learn what hurts them, and contribute to their children's lives, taking time to eat dinner together and really get to know one another.

More than anything, I want all *daddiless* children to know you have a daddy; he is always here and he has always been here. He was there when you were born, hit your first home run, had your first kiss, aced your first test, and even when you fell. He has always been here. Your heavenly father is the one who has kept you throughout all of your trials and tribulations, rich or poor, good or bad; he has been and always will be your daddy. If you believe in him, he will change your life. If you confess with your mouth and believe in your heart that Jesus Christ is Lord, he will change your life. He did it for me and he can do it for you. I would not have been able to overcome the alcohol abuse in my family, my embarrassment from the roaches, and deplorable living conditions, my stubbornness; as well as my shortcomings, without my faith in GOD. I have only accomplished my goals because of his grace.

I sincerely hope this book helps fathers and their children to connect. Maybe these words will be the spark that lights the fire for them to meet and get to know one another. Going through life without being able to identify your father or even knowing where he might be in the world can leave *daddiless* children with unanswered questions for the rest of their lives. I believe it is important for the *daddiless* to establish a connection with their fathers. Even if the encounter between the child and his father is brief, it may allow the two of them to have a sense of closure with regard to his absence. I hope that this meeting will allow the two of them to ask and answer the questions that may have plagued them for years. Neither of them needs to expect anything from the other; I just ask that they both make efforts to recognize one another as people and realize that being *daddiless* can be a *motive* or a *motivation*.

I know there are circumstances when it is best that fathers and their children don't meet. In those cases, I suggest the mother and the children have a dialogue, hopefully to set the record straight and learn why she and their father were not able to make it together. I am also asking mothers to be honest with themselves and with their children so that they can come to know the truth about the circumstances that may have lead to their *daddilessness*.

Families today are suffering in many ways. In most cases, the nuclear family doesn't even exist. Help your children to understand why they are *daddiless*. Help your children to heal and move forward. It is important for fathers to realize that their absence may be one of the biggest *motives* or *motivations* for their children. It is even more significant for these fathers to recognize that, if they have a choice, they should not be absent in the first place. Do not allow your pride or past pain to prevent you from addressing this matter with one another.

It takes special people to move on with their lives after missing such an important part. If you make the right choices and believe in yourself, you can do anything you set your mind to achieve. I am a living example that your situation, rich or poor, does not have to dictate the person that you can become. You can change your situation with determination, perseverance, and a lot of courage. Please be patient with one another because some children and fathers may take longer than others to decide they want to make-up for lost time. Keep your faith in GOD and you can accomplish anything. My heavenly father restored me and delivered me from the bondage that my *daddilessness* kept me in for so many years. His word taught me how to forgive and to overcome. GOD's love filled the void and took away my bitterness. I no longer had to believe I was a bastard child because I have a daddy in heaven. He gives me strength to carry on. You do not have to allow your past to dictate your future. Just believe that he can change your circumstances and you will find peace. Remember to *motivate* yourself and do not rely on others to move you. Listen to the Holy Spirit that dwells within you and he will direct your path. May GOD Bless you and thank you for reading.

www.ingramcontent.com/pod-product-compliance
Lightning Source LLC
LaVergne TN
LVHW051547070426
835507LV00021B/2451